UNTIL
THE WHISTLE
BLOWS

GOODYEAR EDUCATION SERIES

UNTIL THE WHISTLE BLOWS

A Collection of Games, Dances, and Activities for Four- to Eight-Year-Olds

J. Tillman Hall, Ed.D.
Nancy Hall Sweeny
Jody Hall Esser

Goodyear Publishing Company, Inc.
Santa Monica, California

Library of Congress Cataloging in Publication Data

Hall, J. Tillman.
    Until the whistle blows: a collection of games,
dances and activities for four to eight year olds.

    (Goodyear education series)
    Bibliography: p.
    Includes index.
    1.   Perceptual-motor learning.   2.   Educational games.
I.   Sweeny, Nancy Hall, joint author.   II.   Esser, Jody Hall,
joint author.   III.   Title.
LB1067.H27   372.1'3   76-41737
ISBN 0-87620-918-5

Library of Congress Catalog Card Number: 76-41737
ISBN: 0-87620-918-5
Y-9185-3
Current Printing (last number):
10 9 8 7 6 5 4 3 2

Sherri Butterfield, project editor
Louie Neiheisel, designer and art director
Kitty Anderson, illustrator
Thompson Type, typographer

Printed in the United States of America

To Brian and Michelle

ABOUT THIS BOOK

This book is based on the assumption that you—as a parent, youth leader, camp counselor, or teacher—supervise children's play. It is designed to make the task easier for you and the play more meaningful for the children. It is about the proper selection of physical activities for children aged four to eight to provide enjoyment and exercise and to develop physical fitness, positive self-image, sound social behavior, and recreational interest.

PHILOSOPHY

Because life is brief, with much to be learned, it is imperative that all children be given a head start in learning about themselves and their environment. Many reach maturity and are limited in their achievements because they failed to develop specific abilities while they were young. It is extremely important that children between the ages of four and twelve be given maximum help in overcoming deficiencies in motor coordination, in social skills, and in the development of their intellectual capabilities. Many children have a variety of gross and fine motor problems, such as poor coordination, general awkwardness, and defective perceptual acuity. Most of these problems could be arrested or even eliminated through directed play or participation in effective activity and recreation programs. To help you guide children in such play or develop and implement an innovative activity program for your youth group, campers, or class is the purpose of this book.

CONTENTS

This book is divided into eight chapters. Chapters 1 and 2 discuss the physical, emotional, and intellectual needs of children and how some of these needs can be met, correct basic movement patterns established, and desirable skills developed through a formal movement education program, or through less formal activity periods. These two chapters emphasize the importance of identifying your objectives—whether you desire to entertain the children at Jennifer's birthday party, help Michael learn to read by improving his balance, fill a 45-minute period in the campers' day, give the Scouts a chance to blow off steam before settling down to business at their Monday afternoon meeting, develop a ball team, or fill the time until the whistle blows ending the play period.

Chapters 3, 4, 5, 6, and 7 detail, in words, pictures, and diagrams, over 150 games, dances, and activities ranging from finger plays to stunts and tumbling. Within each chapter, the activities are arranged in logical progression from simple to complex and are grouped according to difficulty level. You may need to try portions of several activities to determine where to begin; skill evaluation forms will help you decide when the children are ready to progress to the next difficulty level.

Included in Chapter 5 is a **dance description chart** listing all the dances in the chapter and showing for each the country of origin, the degree of difficulty for four- to eight-year-olds, the basic steps, and the page on which the directions for the dance appear. Detailed dance descriptions include not only the basic steps, formation, and step-by-step instructions, but also a list of records that can be used for the dance. At the end of the chapter is a **list of record sources** containing the names and mailing addresses—categorized by geographical area—of companies from whom these records can be obtained.

So that you may combine these activities in any way you feel is beneficial, they have ordinarily been printed one to a page. Exceptions to this are the Finger Play and Let's Pretend pages found in Chapter 4. Should you wish to locate a specific game or dance, or activities in which a particular piece of equipment (e.g., ball) is used or a specific skill is developed, consult either the **index of activities and terms** or the **index of skills**, both located at the back of the book.

Chapter 8, entitled "The Building Blocks of Physical Life," is an illustrated discussion of the human body and how it knows, grows, and goes. Included are brief descriptions of the skeletal, muscular, cardiovascular, lymphatic, respiratory, nervous, digestive, and endocrine systems, with emphasis upon how these systems affect and/or are affected by exercise, posture, nutrition, and disease or infection. The full-page line drawings in this chapter are designed to be used as is, shown on a screen by means of an opaque projector, or reproduced by making a thermofax master and using a ditto machine to run off the number of copies needed for your group or class. A section on safety and accident prevention concludes this chapter.

FORMAT AND FEATURES

The pages in this book are of **standard notebook size** (8½″ x 11″) to give maximum space for explanations, illustrations, and your notes or observations. The **extra large type** used for the activity descriptions enables you to read and understand them at a glance. The book has been **three-hole punched** so that individual pages or the entire book can be easily stored and used as part of your meeting, lesson, or activity plan notebook, and arranged or rearranged in any order you choose.

The **evaluation sheets** throughout the book and the **anatomical illustrations** in Chapter 8 have been designed to be reproduced. Sheets intended for reproduction, as well as the individual activity sheets, have been marked with **printed cut lines**.

So that you may easily find the activity you need, the brief **back cover contents list** has been arrow referenced to the **chapter number flip indexing** within.

A special feature of this book is the dramatic 30″ x 21″ **poster**. Intended to be both decorative and informative, it shows the major muscles of the body and the antigravity muscles, those that work together to combat the pull of gravity and make standing upright possible.

POSTSCRIPT

Should these activities seem inappropriate for your children, look into the companion volume to this one (purple cover). Written by the same authors for eight- to twelve-year-olds, it not only describes more difficult variations on some of these same activities but also includes chapters on team sports and special programs such as nature study, camping, and crafts.

OUR THANKS TO . . .

Amy, Anne, Brian, Jean, John, Kent, Kirsten, Michelle, Nick, Tara, and Trevor, the kids in the park who helped Kitty create the illustrations.

Bill Call, who took the photographs.

Bobbye Jean Hammond, who typed the final manuscript.

Alice Harmon, Richard Mazzola, and Bobbye Jean Hammond, who helped put the book together.

ABOUT THESE AUTHORS

J. Tillman Hall and his two talented daughters have had extensive experience in teaching children, in traveling with groups of youngsters, and in observing them at play in many parts of the world.

Dr. Hall grew up in a small rural community in West Tennessee. His childhood experiences included many of the recreational activities that interest children everywhere. He excelled in varsity sports in both high school and college, and was active in a variety of school activities, including dramatics, singing and musical groups, social clubs, and intramural games.

After graduation Dr. Hall began his professional career as principal of the elementary school and head coach of all sports at Big Sandy, Tennessee, high school. He served five years in the Navy during World War II, and became coach and head of the Physical Education Department at George Pepperdine College (now Pepperdine University) upon his return from active duty. After earning his doctorate, he was named professor and head of the Physical Education Department at the University of Southern California, the position he currently holds.

He is in the process of writing his ninth textbook, has edited twenty-three books, and has received numerous commendations for his contributions to the education of children from such organizations as the Parent-Teachers' Association, *McCall's*, the City of Los Angeles, Los Angeles County, the California State Legislature, Culver City, California Governor Ronald Reagan, and the Southwest District American Alliance for Health, Physical Education, and Recreation (AAHPER). He is a recipient of the coveted National AAHPER Honor Award and is listed in *Who's Who in the United States*.

Nancy graduated from the University of Southern California (USC) and has done graduate work at USC, California State University at Fresno, and Pepperdine University. She has danced on various television programs and has made stage appearances throughout the fifty states. Her first teaching positions were in Los Angeles and Fresno, California. Later she became head of the primary physical education program for Pilgrim School, a private school for gifted children. She is currently teaching art at Pilgrim School and creative rhythms and outdoor education at the University of Southern California. She is married to Culver City Fire Chief George Sweeny and has two children, six-year-old Brian and nine-year-old Michelle.

Jody graduated from the University of Southern California and has done graduate work at California State University at Northridge (CSUN). She has had extensive experience on stage and in television as both a performer and a choreographer with children and adults. Having taught at CSUN and at Santa Monica City College, she is currently teaching specialized courses in dance and gymnastics and recreation at the University of Southern California. She is married to Jack Esser, a defense systems analyst with Research and Development Associates (RDA).

JODY   DR. HALL   NANCY

CONTENTS

1. CHILDREN'S NEEDS AND HOW THIS BOOK CAN HELP YOU MEET THEM 1

2. PRINCIPLES AND OBJECTIVES OF MOVEMENT EDUCATION 9

3. PERCEPTUAL-MOTOR LEARNING 13

4. CREATIVE MOVEMENT 35

5. RHYTHMS AND DANCE 67

CHILDREN'S NEEDS AND HOW THIS BOOK CAN HELP YOU MEET THEM

1.

Parents, teachers, group leaders, camp counselors—all who work with children must, to some extent, meet the needs of those children, or recognize with regret that they have failed at their task. Some needs do not have to be identified to be met. A certain amount of need satisfaction occurs naturally, unconsciously: children seek out trees to climb without being told, and adults cheer their successes and wipe away their tears without being taught. Other needs, in going unnoticed, also go unmet. Before trying to satisfy them, one must know what they are. One must ask: Exactly, what are the needs of children?

PRIMARY NEEDS

Basic to life itself are food, drink, air, rest, and sleep. These primary needs are somewhat the same for everyone. The amount required may vary, depending on such factors as maturity, physiological efficiency, and intensity of activity; but unless these needs are adequately met, the organism cannot function properly.

SECONDARY NEEDS

Children have a large number of secondary needs, and the degree to which these needs are satisfied often determines how well they adjust to the society in which they live. Fifteen that seem most essential are listed below, with recommendations for meeting them.

1. To acquire knowledge. Children have a desire to learn new truths. They are inquisitive and ask countless questions. This searching, questioning attitude is fundamental to building wisdom. One way to teach children is to direct their natural inquisitiveness with carefully considered questions: Wooden bats are made from what kind of tree? Where does this type of tree grow? How fast does a tree grow? In what city are most bats manufactured? What is a bone? How does it develop? What must I eat to improve bone growth? How many bones does a child have? An adult? What is the purpose of bones? How does the skeleton of a man differ from that of an animal, or an insect? Can bones move by themselves? The answers can be discovered in dictionaries, almanacs, encyclopedias, and other reference books, in school and community libraries, and by "asking the experts."

2. To be creative. Children have a desire to play, to make believe, to build something based upon their own imagination. Rhythm, craft, and drama activities provide creative experiences and aid in developing a "can do" attitude.

3. To belong to a group. Children are gregarious and have a desire to become affiliated with various groups. They like to belong, respond to, be responded to, and be recognized. The group and team activities in this book satisfy this secondary need, "belongingness."

4. To be adventurous. Children have a burning desire to see what is on the other side of the mountain. New experiences, if rewarding, encourage further exploration. Outdoor education, nature study, puzzles, craft classes, and other activities that require some physical skills along with strategic maneuvering help satisfy this secondary need.

5. To be active. The typical child cannot be still very long. It seems as if each cell in his body desires and thrives on exercise. The games and activities in this book will satisfy his present activity needs while developing the muscle tone and coordination required to meet future needs.

6. To be competitive. Most American children are aggressive and desire to match their skills and strategies against those of other children. Properly directed physical activities afford one of the best opportunities to satisfy this need.

7. To be loved. The prepossessing child desires to love and to be loved, to feel wanted, needed, and welcomed. Being included as a necessary member of a group or team in the activities described in this book helps satisfy his need to feel essential.

8. To be successful. Like grown-ups, children desire to be successful. Most of them strive to excell, to be the best, to achieve the most, for which they like to be complimented or rewarded. It is as meaningful for a young child to be awarded a certificate or ribbon for his efforts as it is for an older boy or girl to receive a trophy, sweater, or plaque. Physical activities afford innumerable opportunities for successful experiences, especially if rewards and recognition are liberally given.

9. To feel secure. Children desire to feel safe and to be protected. Games played according to well-defined rules create a feeling of security and build respect for justice and fair play. Meaningful rules that assure good sportsmanship are an American tradition.

10. To manipulate objects. Children have a strong drive to feel and touch objects and to move them from one place to another. This desire can be partly satisfied in playing darts, checkers, chess, and various ball games, and in nature study.

11. To express oneself. Children desire to express themselves vocally, skillfully, rhythmically. Such activities as dance, rhythmic movement, speech, and dramatics afford them an opportunity to do so.

12. To be self-actualized. Self-actualization is a gratifying experience. One progresses toward self-actualization as he strives to realize his full potential, adjusting his goals as the result of learning and motivation. Self-actualization happens when he believes in the adequacy of his learning and in the validity of his value system. A moment of truth occurs during competition when a runner realizes he gave his all but lost to a better performer. He learns to recognize the limits of his ability and to set more realistic goals for himself—or to work harder. Participation in competitive physical activities fosters self-actualization.

13. To be contented. Children have an intense desire to be happy. Their activities should be gratifying, should provide numerous opportunities for pleasure.

14. To be attractive. Children desire to be captivating. To achieve this goal, they must make use of a number of personal qualities, such as cleanliness and hygiene, proper dress and grooming, good posture and physical fitness, personality and their ability to communicate. Well-organized physical activities and recreation programs can develop these qualities.

15. To be physically skilled. Most children desire to participate in various physical activities. Activity skill classes can aid in developing fundamental movement patterns. If motivated to practice, children who have potential may become highly skilled performers.

EDUCATIONAL NEEDS

From time to time agents of a society attempt to identify and list abilities, attitudes, and other forms of behavior which seem to have a positive value in that society. These are then presented in a controlled environment, such as a school, in an attempt to aid children in attaining social competence and optimum development. Perhaps the premier such list was that of the Seven Cardinal Aims of Education:

1. Health
2. Worthy home membership
3. Command of the fundamental processes
4. Vocational training
5. Worthy use of leisure time
6. Citizenship
7. Ethical character

These goals cover the whole of education—and of life itself.

The Educational Policies Commission reduced these aims to the following four fundamental concepts:

1. Self-realization. This process would include developing (1) an inquiring mind; (2) improved skills in speaking, reading, and writing; (3) knowledge of health and disease; (4) improved physical and mental health; (5) skill in participant sports; (6) knowledge of spectator sports; (7) worthy use of leisure time; and (8) aesthetic skills and appreciations.

2. Human relationships. This area encompasses the development of superior human relations, understanding, and appreciation through cooperative play, and would also include courtesy, fair play, and good sportsmanship.

3. Economic efficiency. The aim here is to develop the skills of, an understanding of, and a respect for both the vocational and the consumer aspects of living.

4. Civic responsibility. This concept includes continued growth in understanding and practicing humanitarianism, tolerance, and conservation, in conforming to the law, and in appreciating democratic living.

LEARNING

Learning is generally defined as a change in response or behavior involving some degree of permanence. It results from gaining new knowledge, developing new insights, and/or establishing new skills through the media of study and experience. It is the process by which an idea or activity originates or is changed through experience rather than by growth, development, and maturation.

Learning includes all sorts of changes, such as acquiring a vocabulary, operating a typewriter, and developing prejudices, preferences, social attitudes, and ideals. It tends to improve with practice. Furthermore, it is not necessary to master technical knowledge about the cerebrospinal aspects of learning to know when learning occurs: if something has been learned, it can be repeated, and it is usually measurable.

The speed at which one learns new skills usually depends upon previous learning and experiences, interest in the task to be learned, and maturation. Because children seldom assimilate with permanency more than they understand, it may be necessary to adapt the learning task—activities, games, and the rules by which they are ordinarily played—to their ability level, and perhaps to make a whole game of a single part of an activity.

Regardless of what educational needs one lists and of how learning takes place—and there are nearly as many theories about that as there are people to write about them—the primary purpose of our teaching should be to aid children in developing the skills essential to the accomplishment of present and future tasks. These skills can be classified as cognitive, behavioral, or movement skills.

COGNITIVE SKILLS

Cognition includes all of the intellectual activities as distinguished from conation and affection. It is the mental process by which knowledge, perception, and reasoning occur or are acquired.

BEHAVIORAL SKILLS

Knowledge is regarded as a necessity for wise self-direction, but education should be considered more than the mastery of knowledge: it also includes changes in one's behavior. Such changes may be based on concomitant affective learning, that is, changes in attitudes. Changing attitudes in a multicultural society such as ours may be controversial, but the challenge to do so must not go unmet.

Behavioral skills to be mastered include not only those governing one's relationship with other individuals, but also those essential to one's personal development, such as good study and eating habits, proper exercise, and relaxation techniques.

MOVEMENT SKILLS

Movement skills are learned movement patterns essential to the development of physical efficiency. In their teaching should be reflected the development of the total human movement potential. It takes a baby many months, even with highly individualized tutoring, to learn to roll over, sit up, crawl, pull up, stand, walk, climb, and feed himself. The same kind of guidance and encouragement would be most beneficial in teaching complicated movement patterns to children of elementary school age.

Physical activity periods should be much more than an aimless expenditure of energy or an escape from boredom. As movement or activity education periods, they should be directed, whenever possible, toward the development of desired physical, social, and mental skills, and should encompass activities characterized by

1

maximal enjoyment, good physical exercise, and efficient movement patterns.

Your activity program should include movement skills in each of the following categories:

1. Skills of locomotion
   - Walking correctly (tall, toes straight ahead, one foot always touching the ground)
   - Running (upright, bent over, backward, fast, slow, with both feet off the ground)
   - Jumping (take off on both feet at the same time)
   - Hopping (first on the left foot several times, then on the right foot)
   - Sliding (moving sideways)
   - Skipping (step-hop, first on one foot, then on the other)
   - Leaping (take off on one foot and land on the other)
   - Galloping (One foot reaches in leaping motion. As the other foot is brought up to the lead foot, weight is shifted to it from the lead foot in a short hopping motion. The sequence is repeated rapidly with the same foot leading.)

2. Skills used in assuming a fixed position
   - Lying
   - Sitting
   - Kneeling
   - Squatting
   - Standing
   - Hanging

3. Skills used in playing games and sports
   - Starting
   - Pivoting
   - Stopping
   - Dodging
   - Catching
   - Striking
   - Batting
   - Dribbling
   - Kicking
   - Balancing
   - Vaulting
   - Eye-body coordination

YOUR ROLE

Your role in selecting and teaching physical activities includes defining objectives; organizing materials and equipment; testing, evaluating, and prescribing activities for children; and motivating them to participate and to learn.

Defining Objectives

It has been said that there is no teaching unless some learning takes place. You should have planned objectives and should strive for both general and specific outcomes without excluding the joyful ingredient found in children's play: purposeful activity can be playful.

In 1973 the California State Board of Education adopted a rather comprehensive set of guidelines for physical education. Apparently based on the Seven Cardinal Aims of Education and on the recommendations of the Educational Policies Commission, they differ in that they specifically identify the needs and objectives of physical education. Those that seem relevant for four-to twelve-year-olds are:

1. Basic movement skills should be taught in games and relays in both individual and dual sports, stunts and tumbling, physical fitness activities, rhythmic and dance activities, and team sports.

2. In selecting and teaching physical activities, consideration should be given to cultural needs, including both similarities and differences. When specific activities are repulsive to a given community, they should probably not be included in the program.

1

3. Whenever possible, time should be devoted to improving physical fitness through vigorous activity. (In fact, every able-bodied individual should exercise vigorously, to the point of raising his heartbeat to 125 beats per minute, for at least four minutes each day. He can do so by jogging, running, cycling, or performing various kinds of calesthenics. Maintaining a strong cardiovascular system depends on this kind of exercise.)

4. Physical activity periods should be organized to encourage maximum participation. Enough suitable equipment for practicing specific skills should be made available so that children do not have to wait their turn. Time spent standing in line is wasted and tends to diminish the interest children normally have in being active. All children in the group should be throwing, catching, tossing, running, jumping, dancing, or climbing at the same time—not watching and waiting.

5. Children need instruction in how to develop and improve the following skills:

- Posture—sitting, standing, and moving
- Eye-hand, eye-foot, and eye-body coordination
- Preferred hand and foot, along with bilateral movements
- Awareness of spatial relationships
- Creative expression, self-direction, and independent exploration
- Positive image of self and others
- Appreciation of others in play, work, and study
- Leadership in choosing, demonstrating, and assisting others
- Safety in both work and play
- Understanding the body and how it functions
- Developing and maintaining physical fitness
- Selecting recreational activities that contribute to the worthy use of leisure time
- Foreseeing the consequences of one's actions
- Basic body mechanics for lifting, pulling, pushing, carrying, and supporting various objects

In summary, your physical education or recreation program should include a variety of activities to develop motor skills, physical fitness, self-image, social behavior, and recreational interest.

Teaching activities in sequence according to their difficulty will make it possible for each child to begin at his own proficiency level and progress logically, building each new achievement upon the mastery of its prerequisite skill or skills. The materials in each chapter of this book are arranged in sequential order from simple to complex movement patterns. An occasional review of various recommended activities will often help children perfect movement patterns.

Proficiency in executing movement skills depends on the intensity and frequency of supervised practice sessions. Specific attention should be given to teaching correct movement patterns: ineffective movements, once they have become habitual, are difficult to change.

Keep in mind that, as a child grows, his strength, stamina, coordination, and fine motor skills may vary. He must make a number of complicated adjustments to compensate for relatively small changes in height and weight if he is to repeat certain movements with the same efficiency. Rapid increases in leg length and body weight often result in awkwardness. Special compassion and understanding are needed when this occurs. Children who understand the somewhat mysterious process of growth and development should progress more readily than those who do not and should have greater tolerance for those who seem to move less efficiently; therefore, we encourage you to teach and have the children read about how the body grows, develops, and works, and have included a chapter on this subject at the end of the book.

1

Testing and Evaluating

The extensive use of intelligence, aptitude, and achievement tests may be permanently and adversely affecting the lives and attitudes of many children. Branded as "nonachievers" because of poor test performance, they come to believe they really are inferior to those making higher scores. This is not right, and we know it! Children are more like one another than they are different: the variability is one of degree rather than one of kind. Test scores and evaluations should be used for diagnostic purposes, to determine a child's proficiency level or areas of weakness so that sufficiently challenging or remedial activities can be prescribed, never as a tool to stagnate anyone at any particular level of physical development.

Stimulating and Motivating

Playtime should not be wasted time. In this complex world, there is so much one needs to know that children should not be permitted to learn everything through haphazard personal discov-

ery. Every effort should be made to stimulate each child, to increase his understanding of himself and of the world in which he lives. Successful change entails growth and development. Each child should be encouraged to take part in mind-stretching and body-developing exercises and experiences.

When one participates in an activity, learning is not automatic. There is a definite relationship, however, between the amount one learns and the interest one has in what he is doing. For this reason, considerable effort should be directed toward stimulating eagerness for activities that seem most worthwhile.

One way to motivate interest in physical fitness and skill development is through self-testing. Post score sheets on bulletin boards and have children record the number of times they can repeat an exercise before tiring or making a mistake, the distance jumped, the time in which a specified distance was run, and so forth. Rather than being pitted one against another, the children can be encouraged to better their own scores of yesterday or last week. The following physical skills lend themselves to self-testing:

1. Individual rope jumping (number of times)
2. Sit-ups (number)
3. Push-ups (number)
4. Running (distance, time)
5. Dribbling a ball (with left hand, with right hand, alternating hands)
6. Throwing balls for accuracy and distance
7. Balancing
   - on one leg or the other
   - on the balance beam
   - with a book on the head
   - on a skate board
   - on roller skates
   - on ice skates
   - on a bicycle
8. Jumping (distance, height)
9. Volleying
   - against a backboard
   - in table tennis
   - in tennis
10. Shooting balls through hoops (basketball)

Many other activities can be used for self-testing: this list offers only a brief sample. Given this challenge, children seem to enjoy seeing how many times they can successfully repeat an exercise, and repetition of movements tends to improve their performance.

1

CONCLUSION
Our complex world presents each new occupant with a plethora of stimuli and of challenges. To make sense of the stimuli and to meet the challenges, children must master many cognitive, behavioral, and movement skills; develop and control a number of personal qualities; and alter certain ideas and attitudes. In addition, they have certain needs that must be met, in part, by the society in which they find themselves. A well-designed movement education program can go a long way toward developing the required skills, qualities, and attitudes, and toward meeting many secondary needs. This book outlines such a program. The activities in it are vehicles through which countless concomitant learnings may take place. Your challenge lies in selecting specific activities to meet recognized needs and in presenting them in a manner that motivates children to participate, learn, and develop.

PRINCIPLES AND OBJECTIVES OF MOVEMENT EDUCATION

2.

We have said that a variety of needs can be met and desirable skills developed through a formal movement education program, or through less formal activity periods. Courtesy, fair play, and good sportsmanship can best be learned as a participant in supervised play activities, and participation in such activities enhances a child's ability to make correct judgments.

A large collection of little experiences enriches a child's total experience, and there is practically no end to the activity experiences available to children. Among the possibilities are:

- Playground activities
- Outdoor education projects
- Field trips
- Dramatics
- Arts and crafts
- Camping
- Music, singing, and band activities
- Before and after school activities
- Recess and noontime activities
- Weekend and vacation time experiences
- Club activities
- Individual and team sports

The time and activities are available. What is needed is someone to plan and direct these experiences.

If you are that someone, you will need to consider the principles on which your program will be based and to identify your objectives. Without them, your movement education program or activity period will be haphazard—doomed to mediocrity, or even failure.

PRINCIPLES

A principle is defined as a basic or fundamental truth, law, or assumption on which other truths may depend. In the past, decisions regarding what were the most important things to teach children and what was the best way to teach them were based on principles derived from ex-perience. Though we still depend upon experience in making such decisions today, the current trend is to rely more upon scientific research. The suggestions that follow are supported by both experience and research.

- Learning is proportional to the motivation of the child. Select tasks that afford the greatest opportunity to succeed: success is an important motivational factor.
- Any jackass can kick down a stable door, but it takes a good carpenter to build one: create a good teaching/learning situation. Remove all hazards and unnecessary distractions from the play area. Structure the environment so that the average child can turn in a superior performance.
- Use a positive approach in improving behavior or performance. Avoid belittling children.
- Make every child a winner. Develop the ability to identify and decrease the difficulties children have in learning new skills. Careful placement of children in an activity may enhance their chance for success.
- Keep the learning process challenging, but not overwhelming: break complicated movement patterns down into simple, sequential steps. Teach skills that lead to new skills. When skilled individuals look good while performing, it is because they are in good physical condition and have mastered the sequence of events essential to executing a specific routine.
- When introducing a new activity, discuss briefly but enthusiastically its purpose and importance.
- Children learn motor activities more by imitation than by verbal instruction: demonstrate the activity or select a skillful child to do so, then let *everyone* try it. Always strive for 100 percent participation.
- The rate of learning and the rate of improvement vary from child to child, and readiness **9**

2

may be determined by maturation. Give recognition for trying and for improving, as well as for succeeding.

- Help children discover ways to measure their own achievement.
- Provide opportunities for leadership and fellowship as a member of a group or team. Teach children to value other members of their class, social group, and community at large.
- Promote sociability as well as success in team performance, but help children understand the causes of their failures. Teach them never to be satisfied with second place or with losing if they are capable of capturing first or winning.
- Help children to find themselves, to view their lives as a set of unified experiences. Aid them in appreciating their strengths and in overcoming their weaknesses.
- Encourage children to practice to improve their performance. Remember that an individual rarely reaches the limits of his capacity to improve; however, those in poor physical condition rarely improve quickly.

OBJECTIVES

Objectives are the standards or goals to be sought through movement education or activity experiences. Because each child is stuck with the body he has, he should be taught how it works, how it may be developed, and how it may best be maintained. The more he comprehends, the more likely it is that he will do what is necessary for its healthful maintenance.

The primary objective of any activity or movement education program is to further the participants' development in each of these six areas:

1. Physical Fitness. All children should be taught the dimensions and importance of physical fitness. In reality, it implies having the ability to function at one's very best. One cannot be expected to play any activity well if he lacks the fitness necessary to perform essential movements.

Part of total fitness, physical fitness is a personal attribute influenced by a number of individual factors, including heredity and environment. It is transitory and will disappear unless it is maintained through vigorous exercise.

The major components of fitness are:

- Strength—force a muscle can exert
- Coordination—use of the senses
- Flexibility—maximum range of joint movements
- Stamina—ability to perform repetitive movements
- Speed—ability to move quickly
- Equilibrium—balance
- Power—ability to transfer energy
- Cardiovascular recovery—speed with which the heartbeat returns to normal after exercise is stopped

The physically fit child resists fatigue and disease and has enough resilience to recover quickly from illness or to cope adequately with stress.

2. Motor Skills. Motor skills are reflected in one's muscular coordination and ability during activity performance, and are used in walking, speaking, writing, playing, and manipulating various kinds of objects. Comprehension of perceptual-motor learning, balance, flexibility, general coordination, and mobility is prerequisite to understanding how motor skills are acquired.

3. Health Skills. Nothing is more important than good health. Maximum attention should be given to health concepts, practices, and attitudes with emphasis on safety, posture, relaxation, nutrition, cleanliness, and exercise.

4. Social Skills. Helping children attain social status and make acceptable social adjustments should be a major objective of any program in which children interrelate.

5. Emotional Skills. A large number of cognitive and affective elements intermingle in the development of emotional skills. These elements are judged on a continuum from acceptable to unacceptable. Basic and secondary needs play an extremely important role in emotional development, as do affectional attachments, pleasures, and displeasures.

6. Cognitive Skills. The cognitive skills are the means by which all knowledge is acquired. Together, they constitute the ability to make use of intellectual processes in furthering one's knowledge. They are the faculty of knowing something as distinguished from not knowing it and include, but are more than, intellectual curiosity and problem solving.

BASIC MOVEMENTS

We have good intentions but often demonstrate poor judgment in teaching fundamental movement patterns. Many new patterns are built of existing ones, and their successful performance requires merely transferring old habits to new situations; however, some patterns incorporate new skills. Children find it difficult to acquire new patterns that are based upon skills they have not mastered. For this reason, it is important that basic (part-routine) movements be taught and practiced before full routines are attempted.

Fundamentals are subroutines from which full routines are developed. They include

- the correct way to walk, run, jump, leap, skip, slide, hop, and gallop;
- the correct way to throw, catch, kick, and bounce various kinds of balls;
- good body mechanics, including posture;
- twisting, turning, falling, tumbling, and balance movements;
- a large variety of rhythmic movements;
- manipulative (hula hoop, parachute, bean-bag) activities;
- a variety of health and safety procedures; and
- strategy and tactical play.

The activities described and illustrated in the chapters that follow offer many ways for children to master these fundamentals through supervised play. The evaluation forms that are included will provide you with a way to measure their accomplishment.

UPSIDE-DOWN AND INSIDE-OUT

Movement education has developed through an upside-down and inside-out process. We permit children to move in any way they choose. When they appear to have a natural aptitude or talent for good movements, we select them for a team and teach them the fundamental movements a particular sport requires. By this time, many of them have learned inefficient movements that are difficult to correct.

It would seem more logical to teach all children the correct movements in the beginning. Movement education should be viewed as being fundamental to health and happiness, not simply as a fad or a way to blow off steam. It should be based on sound principles developed through experience and research and should be directed toward achieving particular objectives in body development and skill mastery through both knowledge and practice.

PERCEPTUAL-
MOTOR
LEARNING

3.

Perception can be defined as one's ability to interpret the stimuli around him and to relate them to his own experiences. A child who has good perceptual-motor coordination can coordinate his perception with his movements.

This chapter lists the perceptual-motor tasks a child should be able to perform and explains how to go about helping him learn to perform them. It covers general coordination and locomotor skills, balance skills, eye-hand coordination, and awareness of the body in the space around it. The major emphasis is on helping each child learn efficient movement, develop sensory awareness, and achieve a positive self-image.

The basic equipment needed for the lessons in this chapter includes:
- automobile tires mounted to stand upright
- balance beams of several heights, or one adjustable-height beam
- balls
- beanbags
- bench
- geometric shapes (of wood, paper, etc.)
- hoops
- jumping boxes (8-inch and 16-inch)
- ropes
- traffic cones
- a ladder
- mats
- painted bicycle tires

Because perceptual-motor activities are "fun" and the equipment is often novel, children are usually eager to attempt the tasks, and to repeat them. And each of these lessons is *designed* to be repeated—in whole or in part—many times.

In teaching a lesson, do not hesitate to modify it to fit the abilities of the children involved so that each child may be successful. Make the children aware of the presence of others and of how to avoid collisions or other accidents.

RUNNING ACTIVITIES   10-20 MIN.

Purpose: General coordination, locomotor skill development
Equipment: None
Play Area: Classroom, gym, playground

Directions:
In a well-spaced formation, run
- in a large circle
- in the opposite direction
- with long (short) steps
- very quickly (slowly)
- toward (away from) me
- five steps and walk five steps
- toward (away from) a partner
- with several people

Note:
Allow a rest time between
activities.

Related Activities:
Use this activity to reinforce the
concept of "opposite."

FROM *UNTIL THE WHISTLE BLOWS: A COLLECTION OF GAMES, DANCES, AND ACTIVITIES FOR EIGHT- TO TWELVE-YEAR-OLDS* © 1977 GOODYEAR PUBLISHING COMPANY, INC.

HOPPING ACTIVITIES   5-10 MIN.

Purpose: General coordination, locomotor skill development
Equipment: None
Play Area: Classroom, gym, playground

Directions:

In a well-spaced formation, hop
- on one (the other) foot
- rapidly (slowly)
- taking big (small) steps
- in one place
- high (low)
- toward (away from) me
- toward (away from) a partner
- backward, sideways
- holding your partner's hand

Related Activities:

Talk about animals (e.g., frog, rabbit, kangaroo) and insects (e.g., grasshopper, flea) that hop.

3

JUMPING ACTIVITIES

10-15 MIN.

Purpose: General coordination, locomotor skill development
Equipment: None
Play Area: Classroom, gym, playground

Directions:
In a well-spaced formation, jump
- in a large circle with other children
- in your own small circle
- quickly (slowly)
- high (low)
- toward (away from) me (a partner)
- backward (sideways)
- holding your partner's hand
- with your hands over your head

Related Activities:
- Have the children think of and talk about reasons for jumping (e.g., to clear an obstacle, because one is frightened, to reach an object).
- Hold a sack race.

FROM UNTIL THE WHISTLE BLOWS: A COLLECTION OF GAMES, DANCES, AND ACTIVITIES FOR EIGHT- TO TWELVE-YEAR-OLDS © 1977 GOODYEAR PUBLISHING COMPANY, INC.

GALLOPING ACTIVITIES   10-15 MIN.

Purpose: General coordination, locomotor skill development
Equipment: None
Play Area: Classroom, gym, playground

Directions:
In a well-spaced formation, gallop
- in a circle with other children
- changing lead foot after five gallops
- in your own small circle
- high in the air
- with a partner (hook arms, change)

Related Activities:
Talk about animals that gallop, for example, a pony or horse. Does a giraffe gallop?

3

SKIPPING ACTIVITIES   10-20 MIN.

Purpose: General coordination, locomotor skill development
Equipment: None
Play Area: Classroom, gym, playground

Directions:
In a well-spaced formation, skip
- in different ways
- in a large circle with others
- in your own small circle
- swiftly (slowly)
- high (low)
- in one place
- while you do something with your hands

Make up a pattern of skips and other movements.

Note:
Introduce and have children practice skipping by stepping forward on the right foot and hopping on the right foot, then stepping forward on the left foot and hopping on the left foot: step-hop, step-hop.

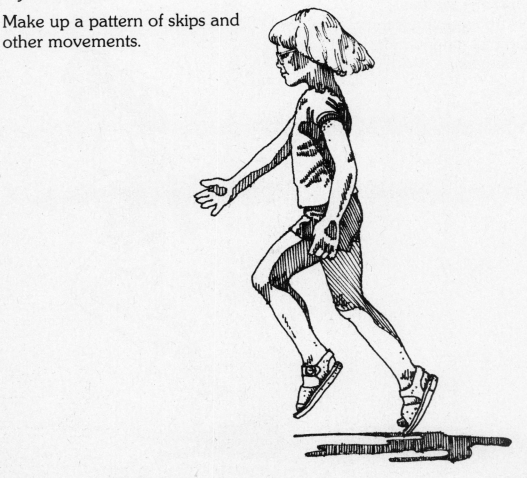

FROM UNTIL THE WHISTLE BLOWS: A COLLECTION OF GAMES, DANCES, AND ACTIVITIES FOR EIGHT- TO TWELVE-YEAR-OLDS © 1977 GOODYEAR PUBLISHING COMPANY, INC.

LADDER ACTIVITIES   10-15 MIN.

Purpose: General coordination, locomotor skill development
Equipment: Ladder, mat
Play Area: Classroom, gym, playground

Directions:

Using a ladder on a mat,
- run between the rungs of the ladder
- walk "on all fours" on the sides of the ladder
- show me another way to go up or down the ladder

Note:

Have each child wait until the child ahead of him has finished his task before beginning.

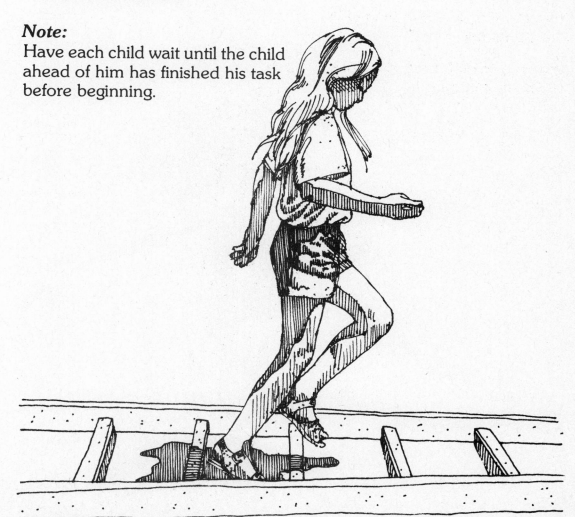

WALKING ACTIVITIES 5-10 MIN.

Purpose: General coordination, locomotor skill development
Equipment: None
Play Area: Classroom, gym, playground

Directions:
In a well-spaced circle or line, walk
- quickly (slowly)
- high (low)
- in a circle with the group
- in your own small circle
- taking very long (short) steps
- by beginning high (low) and finishing low (high)
- from high to low to high

Note:
Keep children well spaced.

FROM UNTIL THE WHISTLE BLOWS: A COLLECTION OF GAMES, DANCES, AND ACTIVITIES FOR EIGHT- TO TWELVE-YEAR-OLDS © 1977 GOODYEAR PUBLISHING COMPANY, INC.

JUMPING BOX ACTIVITIES   20-30 MIN.

Purpose: General coordination, locomotor skill development
Equipment: 3 bicycle tires (1 painted red, 1 blue, 1 green), a jumping box, a mat
Play Area: Gym, playground

Directions:
- Jump from the box and land on the mat with both feet.
- Jump from the box and land in the center of the red (blue, green) tire.
- Jump from the box and land in the red tire. Jump from the red tire to the blue tire, then to the green tire. Jump off the mat.

Note:
Vary the order of the tires and their distance from the box.

Related Activities:
Use this activity to reinforce color recognition and to teach the concepts of "closer," and "farther."

3

EVALUATION

Area: Perceptual-Motor Learning

Skills: General Coordination
Locomotor

Name _____ **Date** _____

Task	Check one or more
1. Walk forward 20 feet.	Movements are smooth ☐ Advances same hand and foot each time ☐
2. Walk backward 20 feet.	Completes task ☐ Stumbles or falls ☐ Wanders in path ☐
3. Run forward 50 feet.	Completes task ☐ Movements are jerky ☐ Arms swing irregularly ☐
4. Jump forward 20 feet.	Completes task ☐ Cannot keep feet together ☐
5. Jump off a 24-inch height and land on your feet.	Completes task ☐ Cannot keep feet together ☐ Afraid of height ☐
6. Hop in place on one foot for 10 seconds.	Completes task ☐ Cannot remain in one place ☐ Must touch floor with raised foot to retain balance ☐
7. Hop in place on your other foot for 5 seconds.	Completes task ☐ Cannot remain in one place ☐ Performs better on one foot than on the other ☐
8. Hop forward 15 feet ☐ on your right foot. ☐ on your left foot.	Completes task ☐ Performs better on one foot than on the other ☐
9. Gallop 30 feet, leading with the foot of your choice.	Completes task ☐ Has difficulty and changes feet ☐
10. Gallop 30 feet, leading with your other foot.	Completes task ☐ Has difficulty and changes feet ☐
11. Skip forward 30 feet.	Completes task ☐ Movements are jerky ☐

3

BALANCE BEAM ACTIVITIES   15-30 MIN.

Purpose: Balance skills development
Equipment: Balance beams of several heights, or one adjustable-height beam
Play Area: Classroom, gym, playground

Directions:
One at a time, while crossing the beam,
- do something on the beam
- walk forward slowly
- walk heel-to-toe
- walk backward slowly
- walk on tiptoes forward (backward)
- slide sideways (reverse)
- hop (jump) forward (backward)
- change levels: sit, kneel, stand
- touch your toes and stand without losing your balance

Note:
Some children may need assistance in stepping on and off the beam.

Related Activities:
Talk about kinds of work (e.g., construction, roof repair) that require good balance.

3

BALANCING ACTIVITIES 1   15-20 MIN.

Purpose: Balance skills
Equipment: Mats
Play Area: Classroom, gym, playground

Directions:
On the floor or a mat,
- stand on one foot (other foot)
- stand on one foot and hold the other ankle (reverse)
- stand on your toes as long as you can (hands on hips, hands clasped overhead, hands on shoulders)
- stand on your toes with your feet far apart (close together)
- move your arms while on your toes
- move them in another way

On a line taped or painted on the floor,
- walk heel-to-toe forward (backward)
- hop to the end on one foot (on the other foot)
- balance on one hand and foot (reverse)

Related Activities:
Talk about animals (e.g., crane) that can balance.

FROM *UNTIL THE WHISTLE BLOWS: A COLLECTION OF GAMES, DANCES, AND ACTIVITIES FOR EIGHT- TO TWELVE-YEAR-OLDS* © 1977 GOODYEAR PUBLISHING COMPANY, INC.

3

EVALUATION

Area: Perceptual-Motor Learning   **Skill:** Balance

Name _____ **Date** _____

Task	Check one or more
1. Stand on the foot of your choice for 5 seconds with your eyes open and your arms held out from your sides.	Completes task ☐ Sways from side to side ☐ Must move weight-bearing foot ☐ "Best" foot is left ☐ right ☐
2. Stand on your other foot for 5 seconds with your eyes open and your arms held out from your sides.	Completes task ☐ Sways from side to side ☐ Must move weight-bearing foot ☐
3. On a 2-inch balance beam or a 2-inch wide masking tape line on the floor, walk a certain number of steps ☐ forward ☐ backward ☐ sideways	Completes task ☐ Steps off board ☐ Pauses often ☐ Must look at feet ☐ Cannot place one foot in front of the other ☐

Additional comments:

3

BEANBAG ACTIVITIES 1   15-20 MIN.

Purpose: Eye-hand coordination
Equipment: 1 beanbag per child
Play Area: Playground, gym

Directions:

In a well-spaced formation,
- throw the beanbag overhand (underhand) to hit a target
- throw and catch alone
- throw and catch with a partner
- catch the beanbag from various distances
- "bounce" the beanbag (What happens?!)

Related Activities:

- Ask and discuss: What is inside a beanbag? Where do beans come from? Name some kinds of beans. What are some other uses for beans?
- Make a picture by gluing beans of various colors on a piece of tagboard, cardboard, or chipboard.

FROM UNTIL THE WHISTLE BLOWS: A COLLECTION OF GAMES, DANCES, AND ACTIVITIES FOR EIGHT- TO TWELVE-YEAR-OLDS © 1977 GOODYEAR PUBLISHING COMPANY, INC.

3

BALL ACTIVITIES 1 20-30 MIN.

Purpose: Eye-hand coordination
Equipment: 1 ball per child
Play Area: Playground, gym

Directions:

In a well-spaced formation,
- throw the ball overhand (underhand) to hit a target
- throw and catch alone
- throw and catch with a partner
- roll the ball to a target
- roll the ball to a partner
- roll the ball with your hands (feet)
- dribble the ball
- kick a stationary ball
- catch the ball from various distances

SHAPE RECOGNITION ACTIVITIES 20-30 MIN.

Purpose: Eye-hand coordination
Equipment: Geometric shapes; paper and pencil for each child
Play Area: Classroom, gym

Directions:

- Show a seated group of children several geometric shapes, one at a time.
- Have them identify each shape orally, then trace that shape in the air.
- Finally, ask the children to draw on paper the shape you name.

Note:

With a small group, try using individual chalkboards.

Related Activities:

- Ask children to name familiar objects composed of different geometric shapes (e.g., STOP sign, octagon; ice cream cone, circle on cone or triangle; house, triangle on square or rectangle).
- Make some simple-shape pictures.

FROM *UNTIL THE WHISTLE BLOWS: A COLLECTION OF GAMES, DANCES, AND ACTIVITIES FOR EIGHT- TO TWELVE-YEAR-OLDS* © 1977 GOODYEAR PUBLISHING COMPANY, INC.

3

EVALUATION

Area: Perceptual-Motor Learning   **Skill:** Eye-Hand Coordination

Name _____ **Date** _____

Task	**Check one or more**
1. Throw a ball overhand 10 to 12 feet.	Completes task ☐ Pattern is smooth ☐ Wrong foot is forward ☐ Uses straight arm ☐
2. Catch on one bounce an 8-inch ball thrown from a distance of 12 to 15 feet.	Completes task ☐ Does not watch ball ☐ Cannot catch ball because of poor hand coordination ☐
3. Stop an 8-inch ball rolled from 10 feet.	Completes task ☐ Eyes do not follow ball ☐ Cannot bring arms together in time to stop ball ☐
4. Draw these figures after being shown them: ☐ circle ☐ square ☐ rectangle ☐ triangle ☐ diamond	Completes task ☐ Pauses in drawing ☐

Additional comments:

3

BODY AWARENESS ACTIVITIES 1   15-20 MIN.

Purpose: Awareness of the body and the space around it
Equipment: None
Play Area: Classroom, gym, grass

Directions:
- Lying on your back, at direction, touch your head, arm, shoulder, neck, knee, foot, ankle, wrist, stomach, fingers, chin, etc.
- Lying on your back, at direction, raise your arm, leg, head, finger, hips off the floor or ground.
- Repeat these exercises while standing, sitting, kneeling, lying on your stomach.
- Sitting (standing), point to the top of your head, back of your head, side of your head (other side), your forehead.

Related Activities:
- This activity may be used to help develop listening skills.
- A logical extension of this activity might be identifying similar (e.g., nose, ears, legs) and different (e.g., wings, tail, fins, feathers) body parts of animals.

FROM UNTIL THE WHISTLE BLOWS: A COLLECTION OF GAMES, DANCES, AND ACTIVITIES FOR EIGHT- TO TWELVE-YEAR-OLDS © 1977 GOODYEAR PUBLISHING COMPANY, INC.

BODY AWARENESS ACTIVITIES 2   15-20 MIN.

Purpose: Awareness of the body and the space around it
Equipment: Traffic cones, bench
Play Area: Gym, classroom

Directions:

- Standing, lean your body forward, backward, to one side, to the other side; twist from one side to the other. Repeat using your head, arms, legs.
- Sitting or standing, point to your left (right) arm, side, foot, leg, cheek, ear, hand, eye, elbow, ankle.
- Stand behind, in front of, beside a traffic cone.
- Walk in a circle, square, etc.
- Go over a traffic cone and under a bench.

Related Activities:

This activity may be used to help
- develop listening skills;
- underscore right-left discrimination;
- teach concepts of direction and relative position (e.g., before, behind, beside, between, in front of).

3

BODY AWARENESS ACTIVITIES 3   20-30 MIN.

Purpose: Awareness of the body and the space around it
Equipment: 2 lengths of rope stretched between 2 pairs of traffic cones, automobile tire upright in a wooden stand; 6-inch or 12-inch walking board, crossbar, beanbag
Play Area: Gym, classroom

Directions:

One at a time, go over the first rope, under the second rope, and through the tire. (Change the position of objects, the height of the ropes, and the order of the directions.)

On a walking board,
- walk forward to end of the board
- walk backward to end of the board
- walk halfway down, then turn around and walk backward to the end
- repeat these activities with a beanbag on your head

After the beanbag and the crossbar are arranged on the walking board, walk forward, pick up the beanbag, and place it on your head. Continue walking, stepping over the crossbar, to the end of the board. (Change the number, order, and type of obstacles.)

Related Activities:

This activity may be used to
- develop listening skills;
- improve the child's ability to follow in correct sequence a series of directions. (Increase the challenge by increasing the length of the series.)

FROM UNTIL THE WHISTLE BLOWS: A COLLECTION OF GAMES, DANCES, AND ACTIVITIES FOR EIGHT- TO TWELVE-YEAR-OLDS © 1977 GOODYEAR PUBLISHING COMPANY, INC.

EVALUATION

Area: Perceptual-Motor Learning   **Skill:** Awareness of Body and Space

Name _____   Date _____

Task	Check one or more
1. Imitation of Movement • Stand with your front (back) side toward me. • Point to your head, shoulders, knees. • Raise one arm; raise the other arm. • Lean forward; lean backward. • Twist your head; tilt your head.	Parallels the patterns ☐ Mirrors the patterns ☐ Hesitates ☐ Moves wrong part of body ☐
2. Obstacle Course (2 chairs and a broomstick) • Slide under the broomstick without knocking it off. (If the task proves too easy, lower the broomstick.) • Step over the broomstick without knocking it off.	Completes task ☐ Knocks bar off ☐ Completes task ☐ Steps too high ☐ Catches foot on bar ☐ Knocks bar off ☐

Additional comments:

3

CREATIVE MOVEMENT

4.

Creative movement is an important aspect of activity programs for young children because it does not involve competition. Instead, it offers each child an opportunity to explore, experiment, and develop his own ways of using his body to solve movement problems, and it makes him feel that any response he gives to a problem is an acceptable one—so long as he does respond.

Your primary goal in leading creative movement activities should be maximum participation. Because all responses are acceptable and much of the equipment is novel, children do not feel intimidated and are usually eager to take part.

Movement problems range from simple to complex. For example, you might give a child a length of rope and say, "Do something with your rope." After he has done something (made a circle on the ground, tied the ends together, tried to jump over it), you might say, "Make a letter with your rope. . . . Now make another letter."

This chapter covers basic movement, story games, finger plays, dramatizations, manipulative activities, rhythmic activities, and creative and imaginative activities. The basic equipment needed for these activities includes:

- balls (1 for each child)
- beanbags (2 for each child)
- hoops (1 for each child)
- jump ropes (1 for each child)
- parachute (round shape preferred)
- record player and records
- rhythm instruments (assorted drums, cymbals, sticks, tambourine)
- scoops (can be made from plastic bleach or water containers)
- tennis-type balls (1 for each child)

Before beginning a creative movement activity,

- establish start and stop signals. You may wish to use a whistle or horn, turn the lights off, or clap your hands. Make a short game of seeing which child or group can respond most rapidly when you give the signal. Establishing such signals will enable you to regain control of the group even if children become overstimulated during the activity.
- demonstrate correct methods for handling and using any unusual pieces of equipment, such as a parachute.
- make children aware of the presence and proximity of others and of how to avoid collisions or accidents.

The activities in this chapter progress from simple to complex. While you may choose and use them singly or in any order, most groups should begin with the first lesson and do the following lessons in order. You may find that you need to modify the tasks to fit the ages and capabilities of your children and to ensure a successful experience for each child.

4

WALKING AND HOPPING ACTIVITIES   5 MIN.

Purpose: Basic movement
Equipment: None
Play Area: Playground, gym

Directions:
Standing an arm's length apart,
- hop from one foot to the other
- walk heel-to-toe from one end of the room to the other
- walk heel-to-toe in a circle or on other shapes taped or painted on the floor

Related Activities:
- Discriminating between circular and linear movement.
- Identifying geometric shapes (square, rectangle, triangle).

4

FROM UNTIL THE WHISTLE BLOWS: A COLLECTION OF GAMES, DANCES, AND ACTIVITIES FOR EIGHT- TO TWELVE-YEAR-OLDS © 1977 GOODYEAR PUBLISHING COMPANY, INC.

BEANBAG ACTIVITIES 2

15 MIN.

Purpose: Manipulative skills
Equipment: 1 beanbag per child
Play Area: Playground, gym

Directions:

In a well-spaced circle,
- throw your beanbag up and catch it
- throw your beanbag higher and catch it
- throw your beanbag ahead and run up to catch it
- toss your beanbag up, turn around in a circle, and catch it
- walk with your beanbag on your head (shoulder, hand)

Related Activities:

- Use this activity to teach and reinforce the concepts of "high–higher."
- Review your discussion of what is inside the beanbag. Where do beans come from? What do we use them for?

4

ACTING OUT A STORY   15-25 MIN.

Purpose: Dramatization
Equipment: Storyteller or record player and record on which a familiar children's story is told
Play Area: Classroom, gym

Directions:

- Select a story or episode from a story with which children are familiar. Consider
    - The Three Bears
    - The Three Little Pigs
    - Peter Rabbit
    - Little Red Riding Hood
    - Cinderella
    - Peter Pan
    - Rumplestiltskin
    - The Shoemaker and the Elves
    - The Ugly Duckling
    - Snow White
    - Sleeping Beauty
- Choose children to act out roles as needed.
- Tell the story or describe the main events in sequence while children act out their assigned parts.

- Repeat the story with different children in each role, or use more than one story so all can participate.
- After several repetitions, choose a child to be storyteller. Let her select the cast and direct the action.

Related Activities:

This activity may be used to teach or reinforce the ideas of sequence and consequence: What will happen next? Why?

4

FROM UNTIL THE WHISTLE BLOWS: A COLLECTION OF GAMES, DANCES, AND ACTIVITIES FOR EIGHT- TO TWELVE-YEAR-OLDS © 1977 GOODYEAR PUBLISHING COMPANY, INC.

HOOP ACTIVITIES 1   10 MIN.

Purpose: Manipulative skill development
Equipment: 1 hoop per child
Play Area: Gym, playground

Directions:
In a well-spaced circle,
- what can you do with your hoop?
- do something else.
- roll your hoop and run alongside it.
- roll your hoop in a straight line.
- spin your hoop.
- roll your hoop in a circle; reverse it.

4

HOOP ACTIVITIES 2

5-8 MIN.

Purpose: Manipulative skill development
Equipment: 1 hoop per child
Play Area: Gym, playground

Directions:

- Do something new with your hoop.
- Spin your hoop.
- Whirl your hoop on different parts of your body (arm, leg, neck).
- Use your hoop as a jump rope.

4

FROM *UNTIL THE WHISTLE BLOWS: A COLLECTION OF GAMES, DANCES, AND ACTIVITIES FOR EIGHT- TO TWELVE-YEAR-OLDS* ©1977 GOODYEAR PUBLISHING COMPANY, INC.

ROPE ACTIVITIES 1

10-20 MIN.

Purpose: Manipulative skill development
Equipment: 1 rope per child
Play Area: Playground, gym

Directions:

In a well-spaced circle,
- what can you do with your rope?
- make a straight line with your rope. Walk the line. Now walk it backward.
- make a circle with your rope. Walk the circle. Walk it backward.
- with your rope in a straight line, jump down one side of it and back up the other side.
- make up a new way to get around the sides of your rope.

Related Activities:

- Ask such questions as: Who uses a rope in his work? (E.g., a cowboy, a stevedore, a tightrope walker.) What does he use it for? (E.g., to catch and restrain cattle, to load and unload ships, to walk on.) How are ropes made?
- Make "rope" by braiding strands of hemp, yarn, or string together, or by using macramé knots.

THROWING AND CATCHING ACTIVITIES

10-15 MIN.

Purpose: Manipulative skill development
Equipment: 1 beanbag per child
Play Area: Gym, playground

Directions:
In a well-spaced circle,
- throw the beanbag up and catch it
- toss the beanbag from one hand to the other
- hold the beanbag between your knees and hop as far as you can
- walk with the beanbag on your head (shoulder, hand)
- close your eyes and toss the beanbag from one hand to the other
- toss the beanbag to a partner and return his toss

Related Activities:
Talk about animals that hop. Do they use two legs or four?

FROM UNTIL THE WHISTLE BLOWS: A COLLECTION OF GAMES, DANCES, AND ACTIVITIES FOR EIGHT- TO TWELVE-YEAR-OLDS © 1977 GOODYEAR PUBLISHING COMPANY, INC.

BALL ACTIVITIES 2

10-12 MIN.

Purpose: Manipulative skill development
Equipment: 1 ball per child
Play Area: Playground, gym

Directions:
In a well-spaced circle,
- do something with your ball.
- toss your ball and catch it.
- bounce your ball and catch it.
- throw your ball and catch it on one bounce.
- dribble your ball. Walk while you are dribbling.

FROM *UNTIL THE WHISTLE BLOWS: A COLLECTION OF GAMES, DANCES, AND ACTIVITIES FOR EIGHT- TO TWELVE-YEAR-OLDS* © 1977 GOODYEAR PUBLISHING COMPANY, INC.

KEEPING TIME TO MUSIC

10 MIN.

Purpose: Rhythmic skill development
Equipment: Record player, records
Play Area: Gym

Directions:
Play records of musical selections
of different tempos and beats.
Have children listen first. Then
have them clap to the music, tap
their feet to the music, walk in time
to the music.

Related Activities:
Associate different musical
selections with different countries.

FROM UNTIL THE WHISTLE BLOWS: A COLLECTION OF GAMES, DANCES, AND ACTIVITIES FOR EIGHT- TO TWELVE-YEAR-OLDS © 1977 GOODYEAR PUBLISHING COMPANY, INC.

ROPE ACTIVITIES 2

5-10 MIN.

Purpose: Manipulative skill development
Equipment: 1 rope per child
Play Area: Gym, playground

Directions:
In a well-spaced circle, can you
- make something with your rope?
- jump rope?
- jump rope with a partner?
- jump rope with more than one partner?
- make a letter with your rope? Another letter?

Related Activities:
- Use this activity to teach or reinforce the skills of alphabet recognition.
- Ask such questions as: Who uses a rope in his work? (E.g., a cowboy, a stevedore, a tightrope walker.) What does he use it for? How are ropes made?
- Make ''rope'' by braiding strands of hemp, yarn, or string together, or by using macramé knots.

PARACHUTE ACTIVITIES 1   15-25 MIN.

Purpose: Manipulative and rhythmic skill development
Equipment: Parachute
Play Area: Gym, playground

Directions:
Before beginning this activity,
- establish stopping and starting signals ("1, 2, 3, lift");
- demonstrate the correct grip (overhand with one or two hands);
- stretch out the parachute on the ground or floor;
- have children space themselves evenly around the parachute, kneel, and grip the chute.

Now tell the children:
- On the count of three, stand up, lift your arms up as high as possible, then immediately bring them and the parachute down and kneel on the edges of it forming a "dome."
- On the count of three, raise the parachute up as you stand up. Step inside it, and pull it down over you to the floor as you return to a kneeling position inside your "cave."
- Holding the parachute with your right (left) hand and pulling it gently toward you, stand and begin walking in a circle around the parachute. Walk more rapidly.

Note:
Be sure to regain complete control and attention before starting a new activity; repeat each activity several times.

Related Activities:
If you have access to music, have children do the walking activity to musical selections of various tempos.

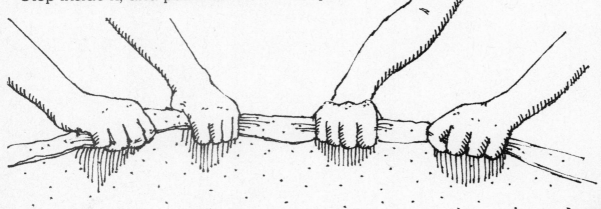

FROM *UNTIL THE WHISTLE BLOWS: A COLLECTION OF GAMES, DANCES, AND ACTIVITIES FOR EIGHT- TO TWELVE-YEAR-OLDS* © 1977 GOODYEAR PUBLISHING COMPANY, INC.

SCOOP ACTIVITIES 1

15-18 MIN.

Purpose: Manipulative skill development
Equipment: 1 scoop and tennis-type ball per child
Play Area: Classroom, gym, playground

Directions:

In a well-spaced formation,
- toss the ball with one hand and catch it in the other hand with the scoop
- toss the ball against the wall and catch it with the scoop
- toss the ball from the scoop toward a target

Related Activities:

What is inside the ball that makes it bounce?

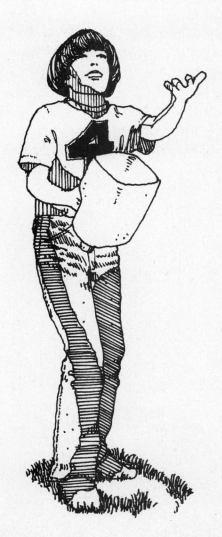

47

MOVEMENTS TO MUSIC

15 MIN.

Purpose: Rhythmic skill development
Equipment: Record player, records
Play Area: Gym, classroom

Directions:

Using records of various tempos,
- walk ⎤
- run ⎥ to the music
- jump ⎥
- leap ⎦

Related Activities:

- Talk about animals that move in various ways.
- When do we run? Walk? Jump? Leap?

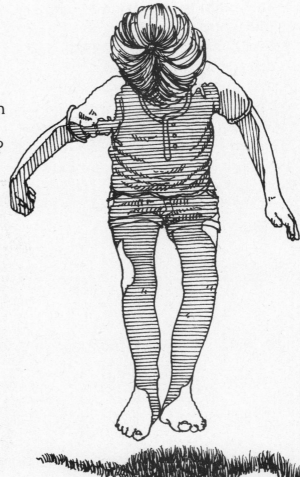

FROM UNTIL THE WHISTLE BLOWS: A COLLECTION OF GAMES, DANCES, AND ACTIVITIES FOR EIGHT- TO TWELVE-YEAR-OLDS © 1977 GOODYEAR PUBLISHING COMPANY, INC.

STRETCHING AND BENDING ACTIVITIES

5 MIN.

Purpose: Basic movement
Equipment: None
Play Area: Classroom, gym

Directions:

- Stretch as tall as you can.
- Make yourself as small as you can.
- Bend as many parts of your body as you can.
- Face a partner and bend (stretch) in the same (opposite) direction.

4

CURLING AND STRETCHING

5 MIN.

Purpose: Basic movement
Equipment: None
Play Area: Gym, playground

Directions:
Lying on your back with plenty of space between you and your neighbor,

- make your body as long (short) as you can.
- bend two parts of your body (two other parts).
- stretch one part of your body; now bend it. (Repeat several times, using another part.)
- make the top of your body touch the bottom.

Related Activities:
- Why do we stretch?
- When do we stretch?

FROM *UNTIL THE WHISTLE BLOWS: A COLLECTION OF GAMES, DANCES, AND ACTIVITIES FOR EIGHT- TO TWELVE-YEAR-OLDS* © 1977 GOODYEAR PUBLISHING COMPANY, INC.

4

BALL ACTIVITIES 3

15 MIN.

Purpose: Manipulative skill development
Equipment: 1 ball per child
Play Area: Gym, playground

Directions:
In a well-spaced formation,
- bounce and catch the ball
- throw the ball against a wall and catch it on the fly
- roll the ball forward, then run ahead and catch it
- roll the ball to a partner and catch it when he returns it
- kick the ball to a partner and catch it when he returns it

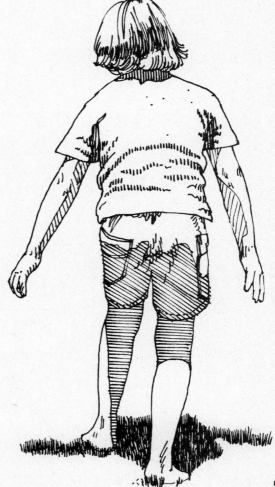

RHYTHMIC ACTIVITIES 1

10-15 MIN.

Purpose: Rhythmic skill development
Equipment: Record player, records of varying tempos and beats
Play Area: Gym

Directions:
Standing in a well-spaced circle,
- clap to a slow beat.
- clap to a faster tempo with underlying beats.
- clap, bend, or walk on a particular beat of the music. (You may want to assign different beats to different groups of children.)

4

FROM UNTIL THE WHISTLE BLOWS: A COLLECTION OF GAMES, DANCES, AND ACTIVITIES FOR EIGHT- TO TWELVE-YEAR-OLDS © 1977 GOODYEAR PUBLISHING COMPANY, INC.

FROM UNTIL THE WHISTLE BLOWS: A COLLECTION OF GAMES, DANCES, AND ACTIVITIES FOR EIGHT- TO TWELVE-YEAR-OLDS © 1977 GOODYEAR PUBLISHING COMPANY, INC.

LIFTING AND LOWERING THE BODY

5-10 MIN.

Purpose: Basic movement
Equipment: None
Play Area: Classroom, gym, playground

Directions:
Standing well spaced,
- raise and lower body parts at direction
- make your body as wide (narrow) as possible
- stand as if you were happy (sad)
- go to a kneeling position

Kneeling well spaced in a crouched position,
- raise your body (one arm, one leg, your head)

Lying well spaced on your stomach,
- raise your head
- raise the right (left) side of your body

Lying well spaced on your back,
- raise your left (right) leg
- raise both legs

Related Activities:
Identifying right and left.

4

PARACHUTE ACTIVITIES 2   15-25 MIN.

Purpose: Manipulative and rhythmic skill development
Equipment: Parachute, 2 or 3 balls
Play Area: Gym, playground

Directions:

Before beginning this activity,
- establish start and stop signals (''1, 2, 3, lift'');
- demonstrate the correct grip (overhand with one or two hands);
- stretch out the parachute on the ground or floor;
- have children space themselves evenly around the parachute, kneel, and grip the chute;
- designate four or more children spaced around the parachute to let go and run under while the others lift.

Now tell the children:
- On the signal, stand and lift the parachute high so other children can run underneath to the other side. Then bring the parachute down. (Repeat this activity until all have had a turn to run.)
- On the signal, stand and raise the parachute, then all let go and run underneath to the other side to bring the parachute down.
- Place several balls in the center of the parachute. Shake the chute and watch the ''popcorn.''

Note:

Regain control before proceeding to the next activity.

FROM *UNTIL THE WHISTLE BLOWS: A COLLECTION OF GAMES, DANCES, AND ACTIVITIES FOR EIGHT- TO TWELVE-YEAR-OLDS* © 1977 GOODYEAR PUBLISHING COMPANY, INC.

BALANCING ACTIVITIES 2　　　10 MIN.

Purpose: Basic movement
Equipment: Mats or grass
Play Area: Playground, gym

Directions:
- With the teacher's aid, stand on your head.
- With a partner, wheelbarrow walk.
- With the teacher's aid, stand on your hands.

Note:
A safe landing is important.

4

RHYTHMIC ACTIVITIES 2

10-15 MIN.

Purpose: Rhythmic skill development
Equipment: Record player, records
Play Area: Playground, classroom, gym

Directions:
In a well-spaced circle,
- skip ⎤
- gallop ⎥
- slide ⎥ — to music
- bend ⎥
- sway ⎦

4

FROM UNTIL THE WHISTLE BLOWS: A COLLECTION OF GAMES, DANCES, AND ACTIVITIES FOR EIGHT- TO TWELVE-YEAR-OLDS © 1977 GOODYEAR PUBLISHING COMPANY, INC.

HOOP ACTIVITIES 3   15 MIN.

Purpose: Manipulative skill development
Equipment: 1 hoop per child
Play Area: Gym, playground

Directions:

In a well-spaced circle,
- whirl your hoop on different parts of your body
- throw your hoop back and forth with a partner
- climb in, out, and around your hoop
- get your hoop to your partner in a new way (by rolling?)

Related Activities:

What shape is a hoop? What other things are that shape? (E.g., wheels, tires, balls.) What motion do they have in common? (They roll.) Can you imagine how it would feel to ride on square wheels?

4

RHYTHM BAND   20-30 MIN.

Purpose: Rhythmic skill development
Equipment: Rhythm instruments; record player and records
Play Area: Gym, classroom

Directions:
- Have children sit in a well-spaced circle.
- Decide who will "direct" (give the signals to start and stop).
- Establish and practice responding to the start and stop signals.
- Use rhythm instruments (drum, cymbals, sticks) in time to music.

Note:
Rotate instruments among children.

Related Activities:
- Discuss how musical instruments are made and how they work. What is *vibration?*
- Make simple musical instruments by stretching rubber bands of varying thicknesses around a shoe box, filling glasses with varying amounts of water, folding tissue paper over a comb, etc.

FROM UNTIL THE WHISTLE BLOWS: A COLLECTION OF GAMES, DANCES, AND ACTIVITIES FOR EIGHT- TO TWELVE-YEAR-OLDS © 1977 GOODYEAR PUBLISHING COMPANY, INC.

4

SCOOP ACTIVITIES 2   20 MIN.

Purpose: Manipulative skill development
Equipment: 1 scoop and tennis-type ball per child
Play Area: Gym

Directions:
Standing well spaced,
- toss and catch your own ball.
- toss or roll the ball to a partner who catches it in his scoop (reverse positions). Start out a short distance apart and gradually move back.
- make up some new ways to play with your scoop.

LET'S PRETEND   UP TO 10 MIN.

Purpose: Imitative and imaginative skill development
Equipment: None
Play Area: Playground, gym

1. *Directions:*

In a well-spaced circle, pretend you are
- on a seesaw
- skiing
- swimming
- skating
- racing
- rowing a boat
- playing football
- playing basketball

2. *Directions:*

With the children seated in a circle, have everyone act out
- washing and ironing clothes
- driving a car
- feeding a baby
- planting something
- flying a kite

Related Activities:

- Ask: Have you ever *really* done these things? Where were you when you did?
- Turn this activity into a simple game of charades. Have one child pretend to be doing something and let others guess what it is. You might wish to limit the activity selection by specifying a category (e.g., water sports, outdoor sports, indoor activities, things you do alone, things you do with a friend, things you do with a team) and/or limit the number of guesses other children may make.

FROM *UNTIL THE WHISTLE BLOWS: A COLLECTION OF GAMES, DANCES, AND ACTIVITIES FOR EIGHT- TO TWELVE-YEAR-OLDS* © 1977 GOODYEAR PUBLISHING COMPANY, INC.

FROM UNTIL THE WHISTLE BLOWS: A COLLECTION OF GAMES, DANCES, AND ACTIVITIES FOR EIGHT- TO TWELVE-YEAR-OLDS © 1977 GOODYEAR PUBLISHING COMPANY, INC.

3. *Directions:*
In a well-spaced circle, pretend you are
- an ape
- a cat
- a duck
- an elephant
- a giraffe
- a horse
- a kangaroo
- a rabbit
- a snake

Related Activities:
Discuss where each animal lives, and what he eats. Is he a *carnivore?* A *herbivore?* An *omnivore?*

4. *Directions:*
With the children seated in a circle, choose several children to pretend to be
- witches
- dragons
- monsters

4

FINGER PLAYS   UP TO 5 MIN.

Purpose: Relaxation and imitative skill development
Equipment: None
Play Area: Anywhere

1. BEFORE I CROSS THE STREET
Directions:
While children are sitting in chairs or cross-legged on the floor or ground, have them say and act out this rhyme with you:

Words	Actions
Before I cross the street,	
I look up the street,	Turn your head to look in one direction.
And down the street.	Turn your head to look in the opposite direction.
First I use my eyes.	Point to your eyes.
Then I use my ears.	Point to your ears.
Then I use my feet.	Mark time or point to your feet.

Related Activities:
Discuss how to cross streets safely.

2. ME
Directions:
While children are sitting in chairs or cross-legged on the floor or ground, have them say this rhyme with you and point to the body part named.

Here are my eyes and here is my nose.
Here are my fingers and here are my toes.
Here are my eyes, both open wide.
Here is my mouth with my teeth inside.
Here is my chin and here is my cheek
And my busy tongue that helps me speak.
Here are my hands that help me play
And my feet that run around all day.

FROM *UNTIL THE WHISTLE BLOWS: A COLLECTION OF GAMES, DANCES, AND ACTIVITIES FOR EIGHT- TO TWELVE-YEAR-OLDS* © 1977 GOODYEAR PUBLISHING COMPANY, INC.

3. THE WITCH

Directions:

While children are sitting or standing where they can see you, have them say this rhyme and follow your motions.

Words	Actions
I saw a witch	
In a tall peaked hat,	Make the outline of a "tall peaked
Riding a broom	hat" above your head.
With a coal black cat.	
I saw a witch,	
But she didn't see me,	Shake your head "no."
For I was hiding	
Behind a tree!	
When she went by,	
I jumped out and yelled, "Boo!"	
And my was she frightened!	
And away she flew!	Make your fingers "fly" away from your body.
She left her broom	Repeat "peaked hat" gesture.
And her tall peaked hat,	
And her painted mask	
And her coal black cat.	
I don't know when	
I've had such fun	
As on Halloween night	
When I made a witch run!	

4

63

4

4. I HAVE TEN LITTLE FINGERS

Directions:
While children are sitting in chairs or cross-legged on the floor or ground,
have them say this rhyme with you and follow your finger motions.

I have ten little fingers,
And they all belong to me.
I can make them do things.
Would you like to see?

> *I can shut them up tight,*
> *Or open them wide.*
> *I can put them together,*
> *Or make them all hide.*

> *I can make them jump high.*
> *I can make them jump low.*
> *I can fold them up quickly,*
> *And hold them just so.*

FROM *UNTIL THE WHISTLE BLOWS: A COLLECTION OF GAMES, DANCES, AND ACTIVITIES FOR EIGHT- TO TWELVE-YEAR-OLDS* © 1977 GOODYEAR PUBLISHING COMPANY, INC.

5. SOLDIERS

Directions:

While children are sitting in chairs or cross-legged on the floor or ground, have them say this rhyme with you and follow your finger motions.

Words	Actions
Four little soldiers standing in a row,	Hold up four fingers.
Two stood straight and two stood so.	Hold two up straight; bend two.
Along came the general,	Hold up the thumb
And what do you think?	on your other hand.
They all stood up straight	Straighten the two bent fingers
Quick as a wink!	so that all four are straight.

RHYTHMS AND DANCE

5.

This chapter covers creative rhythmic activities and simple recreational folk dances. Such activities aid children in developing creative self-expression; body control, awareness, and coordination; and the ability to "work" with a partner or as part of a group.

For children aged four through seven, emphasis should be primarily on creative expression and the development of rhythmic skill fundamentals, including locomotor movements, rhythm identification and reproduction, and basic dance steps, formations, and positions. With children eight years old and older, more emphasis can be placed on learning set patterns of dance steps and on refining rhythmic movements.

The activities in this chapter are arranged from simple to complex. Evaluation forms interspersed among chapter activities should help you decide the level at which to begin.

RHYTHMIC/MUSICAL ACCOMPANIMENT

Rhythmic or musical accompaniment, whether in the form of a tom-tom or dance drum, record, tape, piano, song, or poem, should be appropriate to the activity and characterized by good sound reproduction. It should also stimulate children to move.

In the beginning it may be easier to use self-accompaniment (drum, tambourine, songs, spoken phrases). In addition, many of the creative exploration recordings available are excellent for practice and development of basic movement skills and dance steps. Recordings of musical accompaniment for specific dances are listed with each activity.

Reproducing rhythmic beats on their own instruments will help children comprehend the elements of rhythm. Simple handmade instruments, including drums, sticks, sandpaper blocks, and bean boxes, may be used for this purpose.

ELEMENTS OF RHYTHM

Tempo—The speed of the music or beat.

Beat—The underlying rhythmic quality of the accompaniment, either uneven or even in presentation.

Meter—The combination and manner of organization of beats to form a measure. Combinations of meters used in rhythm are called *time signatures* and indicate the number of beats found in a measure and what note receives one beat.

Example: 2 = beats per measure
4 = a quarter note receives one beat

Common time signatures are:

$\frac{2}{4}$ polka

$\frac{3}{4}$ waltz

$\frac{4}{4}$ schottische, march

$\frac{6}{8}$ two-step

Accents—The notes or beats that are emphasized.

Intensity—The force of the accompaniment (loud, soft, heavy, light).

Mood—The feeling displayed by the accompaniment (happy, sad, lazy, busy).

Phrase—The pattern or grouping of measures. Commonly, phrases are groupings of 8 or 16 measures.

Patterns—The arrangement of phrases in the music (chorus, verse).

In teaching the elements of rhythm to children,
- give ample opportunities for listening to, discussing, and reproducing beats;
- provide opportunities to clap, tap, walk, run, skip, and hop in time to a rhythmic beat;

5

- discuss and note changes in the elements of rhythm (accented beats or words, mood feeling of sounds, phrasing—where the chorus stops, where the verse begins).

Development of a sense of rhythm depends on opportunities for expression and practice.

CREATIVE RHYTHMS

Allowing the children to express freely their emotions, impressions, and feelings fosters their creative abilities. Successful creative rhythmic activities

- emphasize that movement expression is both feminine and masculine;
- encourage self-generated expression as opposed to following directions;
- provide opportunities for problem solving and discussion of decisions and alternatives;

- provide opportunities for movement relevant to the child's understanding of topic ideas and directions before the activity begins.

DANCE

Before learning dances, children should develop and perfect basic locomotor movements and directional concepts, and should perform these fundamentals in various formations. They should learn these fundamentals through a progressive series of directed experiences that teach elements of rhythm along with movement skills, and make them aware of music phrasing, position placement (spacing), and identification and reproduction of various rhythms.

5

Terms

Balance—Step toward partner with one foot, touch toe of other foot alongside. Reverse to original place.

Bleking step—Step forward on one foot, sweep other foot across shin of stationary leg, and do small hop-step in place at same time.

Bow—Boy bends forward from waist, keeping legs straight and folding right arm across waist in front, left arm across waist in back.

Curtsy—Girl steps to right side with right foot, touches left foot behind right, and bends knees, torso, and head slightly as to nod.

Draw step—Step to side with one foot and draw up other foot to touch at side.

Elbow swing—Partners hook either right or left elbows and walk, run, skip, or hop in a circle.

Face-to-face, back-to-back step—Partners facing, boy holds girl's left hand in his right. Boy on left foot, girl on right, perform slide-close-slide hop-step sideways (counterclockwise), swing arms forward, pivot on hop half turn. Repeat step back-to-back, swing arms backward, pivot to face partner.

Heel-toe step—Hop and extend right foot to side with toe pointed up. Hop again, keeping right foot extended and point toe to ground.

Inside foot—In single formation, the foot closest to circle center when facing either clockwise or counterclockwise; for couples, the foot closest to partner when both are facing clockwise or counterclockwise.

Outside foot—In single formation, the foot farthest away from circle center when facing clockwise or counterclockwise; for couples, the foot farthest away from partner when standing side by side facing clockwise or counterclockwise.

Polka—Hop on right foot, step forward on left, close right to left, step on left. Repeat, starting with hop on left foot.

Schottische—Walk forward right, left, right, and hop on right foot; walk forward left, right, left, and hop on left foot.

Step-hop—Step on right foot, hop in place on right foot. Step on left foot, hop in place on left foot.

Toe-heel step—Standing on left foot, point right toe to ground alongside left, step on right. Standing on right foot, point left toe to ground alongside right foot, step on left.

Two-step—(Described as performed in place, moving from side to side.) Step left, close right, step left touch right toe alongside left. Step right, close left, step right, touch left toe alongside right. Step can also be performed moving forward and backward.

5

Basic Formations

Double circle with partners facing; boys
standing with backs to circle center.

Double circle with partners
facing either clockwise (pictured)
or counterclockwise, or with sets
of partners facing.

5

Single circle facing either center, clockwise (pictured), or counterclockwise.

Single circle with partners facing one another.

Positions

Inside hands held.

Arms around waists.

Skaters' position: partners stand side by side, extend inside arms to hold left to left hand, right to right hand.

5

Two hands held.

Shoulder-waist position: boy's hands on girl's waist; girl's hands on boy's shoulders.

Social dance position: boy's right hand on girl's waist, left hand extended; girl's left hand on boy's shoulder, right hand extended.

Varsouvienne position: boy stands slightly behind girl and extends arms to sides; girl extends arms to join boy's hands.

73

EXPLORING BASIC MOVEMENTS

Introduction: A wide variety of locomotor, nonlocomotor, and manipulative movements provide the foundation for rhythmic and dance activities. These locomotor movements include walking, running, skipping, hopping, leaping, sliding, galloping, and jumping. The nonlocomotor movements include swinging, bending, stretching, falling, turning, rolling, and crawling. The manipulative movements include striking, throwing, pushing, pulling, lifting, hammering, and ball handling.

Encourage children to spread out and to watch for others. Use descriptive words to encourage movement. Change movement directions frequently so children don't tire of the exploration. Make sure the children can perform the skill (hop, jump, leap, etc.) before calling for it. Demonstrate, then have them try it.

Directions:

Walk
- like giants
- on tiptoes
- like fairies
- using little steps
- using big steps
- like soldiers
- like a robot

Run
- as if someone is chasing you
- slowly, as if you are tired
- forward
- backward
- like an elderly person

Skip
- for fun
- like a happy person
- slowly
- lifting up in the air
- quickly

Hop
- like a bunny rabbit
- on one foot, then on the other
- like a rag doll
- like a kangaroo

5

FROM *UNTIL THE WHISTLE BLOWS: A COLLECTION OF GAMES, DANCES, AND ACTIVITIES FOR EIGHT- TO TWELVE-YEAR-OLDS* © 1977 GOODYEAR PUBLISHING COMPANY, INC.

Leap
- over a puddle
- over a hedge
- over a rock

Slide
- in a circle
- slowly
- quickly
- on tiptoes

Gallop
- like a pony
- like a cowboy
- following the leader

Jump
- like a bouncing ball
- like a bird
- like a frog

Swing
- like a leaf on the wind
- like a swing
- like a tree

Turn and Twist
- like an airplane
- like a top
- like a snowflake
- like a leaf in the wind

Push Pull
- like you are in a tug-of-war
- like you are raking leaves
- like you are mowing the lawn

Strike
- like you are beating a drum
- like you are hammering a nail
- like you are chopping wood

5

Bend
- like you are picking flowers
- forward and back
- like a rocking horse

Fall
- gently like a leaf in the wind
- slowly like a snowflake
- loosely like a rag doll.

Related Activities:
Use these motor and nonmotor movements to act out a story or theme. Consider nursery rhyme and storybook characters, holidays, animals, trips to the zoo, hunting, fishing, firemen, policemen, bus drivers, parties, and family members. Be sure the children understand the story and words denoting movement.

CREATIVE RHYTHMIC MOVEMENT

Introduction: To encourage free expression, interpretation of movement, and a sense of rhythm, an element of self-expression should be found in every movement session. Specialized recordings for rhythmic movement and rhythm identification include:

Title	Writer/Producer	Number
Primary Musical Games	Educational Activities, Inc.	HYP 23
Basic Rhythms	Educational Activities, Inc.	HYP 7
Play Party Games, Singing Games, Folk Dances	Educational Activities, Inc.	HYP 10
Fun Activities for Fine Motor Skills	Kimbo Educational	LP 9076
Develop Motor Skills for Self Awareness	Kimbo Educational	LP 9075
The Feel of Music	Educational Activities, Inc. Hap Palmer Record Library	AR 556 or AC 556*
Ideas, Thoughts and Feelings	Educational Activities, Inc. Hap Palmer Record Library	AR 549 or AC 549
Getting to Know Myself	Educational Activities, Inc. Hap Palmer Record Library	AR 543 or AC 543
Creative Movement and Rhythmic Exploration	Educational Activities, Inc. Hap Palmer Record Library	AR 533 or AC 533
Home Made Band	Educational Activities, Inc. Hap Palmer Record Library	AR 545 or AC 545
Movin'	Educational Activities, Inc. Hap Palmer Record Library	AR 546 or AC 546
Holiday Songs and Rhythms	Educational Activities, Inc. Hap Palmer Record Library	AR 538 or AC 538
Readiness Albums Rainy Day Record	Educational Activities, Inc. By Glass and Hallum	AR 533 or AC 533
Dance a Story	RCA Victor	LPMs LE 101-108
To Move and To Be	Kimbo Educational and Educational Activities, Inc. By JoAnn Seker	KEA 8060
Movement Rhythms Movement Exploration	Kimbo Educational	KIM 3090
Music for Creative Movement	Kimbo Educational By Carol Lee	Vol. 1, KIM 6070 Vol. 2, KIM 6080
Come Dance with Me	Hoctor Records	

*AC denotes cassette number.

When playing various music selections, have the children listen to the beat, clap to the beat, walk-run to the beat, tap toes to the beat. Encourage good listening and beat identification.

FROM UNTIL THE WHISTLE BLOWS: A COLLECTION OF GAMES, DANCES, AND ACTIVITIES FOR EIGHT- TO TWELVE-YEAR-OLDS © 1977 GOODYEAR PUBLISHING COMPANY, INC.

Directions:

- Present a rhythmic sound-beat for listening and let each child decide how he wants to act out what the rhythm makes him think of.
- Have the children decide what they want to act out or be and find a suitable accompaniment. You may need to make suggestions to get them started.
- Have the children listen to one or several selections of music and decide which one they choose to "act out."

Related Activities:

- Discuss what the music makes the children think of.
- Discuss ideas and characters for acting out.
- Review and increase basic motor skills.

5

SINGING GAMES

Directions:
- Learn the music and verse to the song.
- Tell something about the nature or meaning of the song.
- Analyze the music. Listen to the beat and tempo. Have the children clap, tap, nod, or walk to the music.
- Add the actions.
- Repeat two or three times.
- Repeat singing games that have become familiar fairly often for recall. Vary original actions as time passes.

AROUND WE GO

Sung to the tune of: Lazy Mary, Will You Get Up?
Formation: Children in a circle, hands clasped, walking.

Words	Actions
Around we go, around we go *One big circle marching so.*	Walk in a circle.
Down we go, down we go *One big circle sinking so.*	Walk bending knees.
Up we go . . . rising so. *In we go . . . shrinking so.* *Out we go . . . stretching so.*	Walk on tiptoes. Walk toward center of circle. Walk backward from circle center.

FROM UNTIL THE WHISTLE BLOWS: A COLLECTION OF GAMES, DANCES, AND ACTIVITIES FOR EIGHT- TO TWELVE-YEAR-OLDS © 1977 GOODYEAR PUBLISHING COMPANY, INC.

5

BAA, BAA, BLACK SHEEP

Sung to the tune of: Baa, Baa, Black Sheep
Formation: Free formation, children scattered.

Words

Baa, baa, black sheep,
Have you any wool?

Yes, sir, yes, sir,
Three bags full:

One for my master,
And one for my dame,

And one for the little boy
Who lives down the lane.

Actions

Pretend to be sheep, placing fingers beside head for horns, and prance.

Nod head on "yes" and hold up three fingers.

Hold up one finger on "one."

Hold up one finger on "one."

ON THIS RAINY DAY

Sung to the tune of: Mary Had a Little Lamb
Formation: Sitting, scattered.

Words

Everybody clap your hands,
Clap your hands,
Clap your hands.

Everybody clap your hands
On this rainy day.

. . . tap your toes
. . . stretch and stand
. . . rest a while
. . . sit in place

Actions

Follow directions of words.

Note: Substitute *sunny* day or *snowy* day for rainy day if you choose.   79

Other Songs for Singing Games

- Itsy Bitsy Spider
- Old King Cole
- Brother John
- Diddle, Diddle Dumpling
- Yankee Doodle
- Twinkle, Twinkle, Little Star
- Hay, Ho Halloween's Here
- Mary Had a Little Lamb
- Who's That Knocking at My Door?
- Good Morning
- Jack Be Nimble, Jack Be Quick

5

FROM UNTIL THE WHISTLE BLOWS: A COLLECTION OF GAMES, DANCES, AND ACTIVITIES FOR EIGHT- TO TWELVE-YEAR-OLDS © 1977 GOODYEAR PUBLISHING COMPANY, INC.

EVALUATION

Area: Rhythms and Dance
Skill: Basic Rhythm Identification

Name _____ **Date** _____

Task	Check one or more
1. Clap to music.	In rhythm ☐ Not in rhythm ☐
2. Walk to music as tempo is varied gradually.	In rhythm ☐ Can stay with tempo change ☐ Unsure of rhythm, watching others ☐

Additional comments:

EVALUATION

Area: Rhythms and Dance
Skill: Basic Rhythm Identification

Name _____ **Date** _____

Task	Check one or more
1. Clap to music.	In rhythm ☐ Not in rhythm ☐
2. Walk to music as tempo is varied gradually.	In rhythm ☐ Can stay with tempo change ☐ Unsure of rhythm, watching others ☐

Additional comments:

DANCES

Dance Description Chart

Name of Dance	Country of Origin	Degree of Difficulty	Basic Steps	Page
The Farmer in the Dell	England	Very easy	Walk	84
Baa, Baa, Black Sheep	England	Very easy	Walk, stamp, turn	85
Here We Go Round the Mulberry Bush	England	Very easy	Walk or skip	86
Let Your Feet Go Tap, Tap, Tap	USA	Very easy	Skip	87
Pease Porridge Hot	England	Very easy	Skip, clap	88
Looby Loo	England	Very easy	Skip, body actions	91
Seven Jumps	Denmark	Easy	Slide	92
Dance of Greeting	Denmark	Easy	Bow, stamp, run	93
Chimes of Dunkirk	France	Easy	Skip, stamp	94
The Wheat	Czechoslovakia	Easy	Walk, skip, partner turn	95
Pop Goes the Weasel	USA	Easy	Walk, balance	96
Bingo	USA	Easy	Walk, grand right and left	99
Shoemaker's Dance	Denmark	Moderate	Skip	100
Carrousel	Sweden	Moderate	Slide, stamp	101
Indian Rain Dance	USA	Moderate	Toe-heel step	102
The Crested Hen	Denmark	Moderate	Step-hop	105
Bleking	Sweden	Moderate	Bleking step	106
La Raspa	Mexico	Moderate	Bleking step	107
Kinderpolka	Germany	Moderate	Step-close	108
Korobushka	Russia	Moderate	Schottische, balance	109
Come Let Us Be Joyful	Germany	Moderate	Walk, skip	110

5

THE FARMER IN THE DELL
ENGLAND

Basic Step: Walk
Record: Victor 21618, Victor 45-5066
         (Album WE87), Folkraft 1182
Formation: Circle, hands clasped.

Directions:

- Choose one child to be the "farmer" and stand in the center of the circle. Other children walk in a circle, clockwise.
- As the farmer chooses a wife, a child, etc., chosen players move to the center of the circle. Remaining children close their circle to clasp hands where chosen child was.

- After wife, child, nurse, dog, cat, mouse, and cheese are chosen and in the center, all return to their places in the circle except "cheese," who "stands alone" in the center of the circle while other players face the center, sing, and clap their hands.

5

84

FROM UNTIL THE WHISTLE BLOWS: A COLLECTION OF GAMES, DANCES, AND ACTIVITIES FOR EIGHT- TO TWELVE-YEAR-OLDS © 1977 GOODYEAR PUBLISHING COMPANY, INC.

BAA, BAA, BLACK SHEEP   ENGLAND

Basic Steps: Walk, stamp
Records: Folkraft 1191, Russell 700A, Victor E-83
Formation: Single circle, facing center.

Words

Baa, baa, black sheep,
Have you any wool?

Yes, sir, yes, sir,
Three bags full:

One for my master,
And one for my dame,

And one for the little boy
Who lives down the lane.

Actions

Stamp three times. Shake forefinger three times.

Nod head twice and hold up three fingers.

Bow to the person on the right, then to the person on the left.

Hold up one finger, and turn singly in circle, ending facing center.

Related Activities:

• Where is England?
• What games do children play there?
• What is the weather like?

5

HERE WE GO ROUND THE MULBERRY BUSH

ENGLAND

Basic Steps: Walk or skip
Records: Victor 20806, 45-5065, Columbia 90037-V, Folkraft 1183
Formation: Single circle, hands clasped, facing center.

Directions:

- The dance begins with the chorus, and the chorus is repeated after each verse.
- During the chorus, children walk (or skip) to the right 12 steps. On the last 4 ("so early in the morning"), they drop hands and turn all the way around in place, to end facing the center of the circle.

- During the verse, children act out words ("wash the clothes, . . . iron the clothes, . . . mend the clothes, . . . sweep the floor, . . . scrub the floor, . . . make a cake, . . . go to church"), changing the day of the week in each verse ("all on a Monday . . . Tuesday . . . Wednesday . . . morning").

FROM UNTIL THE WHISTLE BLOWS: A COLLECTION OF GAMES, DANCES, AND ACTIVITIES FOR EIGHT- TO TWELVE-YEAR-OLDS © 1977 GOODYEAR PUBLISHING COMPANY, INC.

5

LET YOUR FEET GO TAP, TAP, TAP

USA

Basic Step: Skip
Record: Folkraft 1184
Formation: Double circle, partners facing.

Words	Actions
Verse:	
Let your feet go tap, tap, tap.	Tap one foot three times.
Let your hands go clap, clap, clap.	Clap hands three times.
Let your fingers beckon me.	Beckon with finger and bow to partner.
Come, dear partner, dance with me.	Join hands and face counterclockwise.
Chorus:	
Tra, la, la, la, la, la, la.	Sing and skip counterclockwise.

5

PEASE PORRIDGE HOT   ENGLAND

Basic Steps: Skip, clap, turn in an individual circle
Record: Folkraft 1190
Formation: Double circle, partners facing.

Directions:
Verses must be repeated twice to complete dance.

Words	Actions
Pease porridge hot.	Slap thighs, clap own hands together, slap partner's hands.
Pease porridge cold.	Slap thighs, clap own hands together, slap partner's hands.
Pease porridge in the pot	Slap thighs, clap own hands together, slap right hand to partner's right hand, clap own hands together.
Nine days old.	Slap left hand to partner's left hand, clap own hands together, slap both partner's hands.
Some like it hot.	Slap thighs, clap own hands together, slap partner's hands.
Some like it cold.	Slap thighs, clap own hands together, slap partner's hands.
Some like it in the pot	Slap thighs, clap own hands together, slap right hand to partner's right hand, slap left hand to partner's left hand.
Nine days old. Repeat.	Slap partner's hands three times. Join hands with partner. Skip in counterclockwise circle 16 times. Skip 16 times in the opposite direction. Dancers end in original position and take one step to the left to new partner.

FROM *UNTIL THE WHISTLE BLOWS: A COLLECTION OF GAMES, DANCES, AND ACTIVITIES FOR EIGHT- TO TWELVE-YEAR-OLDS* © 1977 GOODYEAR PUBLISHING COMPANY, INC.

5

Other Dances Suggested for This Level
- Ten Little Indians—*Folkraft 1197*
- Muffin Man—*Folkraft 1188*
- London Bridge—*Victor 20806*
- Gay Musician—*Folkraft 1185*

5

EVALUATION

Area: Rhythms and Dance
Skills: Rhythm Identification
Walking, Skipping

Name _____ Date _____

Task	Check one or more
1. Walk to music; change direction.	Moves in time to music ☐ Does not move in time to music ☐
2. Skip to music.	Moves in time to music ☐ Does not move in time to music ☐

Additional comments:

EVALUATION

Area: Rhythms and Dance
Skills: Rhythm Identification
Walking, Skipping

Name _____ Date _____

Task	Check one or more
1. Walk to music; change direction.	Moves in time to music ☐ Does not move in time to music ☐
2. Skip to music.	Moves in time to music ☐ Does not move in time to music ☐

Additional comments:

LOOBY LOO   ENGLAND

Basic Step: Skip
Records: Victor 20214, Russell 702, Columbia 10008D, Folkraft 1102, 1184
Formation: Single circle, all facing center, hands clasped.

Directions:
The dance begins with the chorus, which is then repeated after each verse.

Words	Actions
Chorus:	
Here we go looby loo.	Hold hands and
Here we go looby light.	skip counterclockwise.
Here we go looby loo	
All on a Saturday night.	
Verse:	
1. I put my right hand in.	Follow directions
I take my right hand out.	of words.
I give my right hand a shake,	
shake, shake,	
And turn myself about.	Turn completely around, then join hands for chorus.
2. . . . left hand in . . .	
3. . . . right foot in . . .	
4. . . . left foot in . . .	
5. . . . right hip in . . .	
6. . . . left hip in . . .	
7. . . . head in . . .	
8. . . . whole self in . . .	

Variation:
This dance is very similar to the
Hokey Pokey (MacGregor 669A)

5

SEVEN JUMPS   DENMARK

Basic Step: Sliding
Records: RCA LPM 1623, World of Fun 108
Formation: Single circle, hands joined, facing center.

Directions:
To musical cues, first perform the chorus, then the verse, and then the chorus again. Notice that, with each successive verse, a new action is added to the old ones, which are repeated in the order in which they were introduced.

Steps	*Measures*
Chorus:	
Slide 7 times to the right.	**16**
Jump on eighth count.	
Stop in place.	
Slide 7 times to the left.	
Jump on eighth count.	
Stop in place.	

Verse:
1. Raise right knee. Lower right knee. Hold one measure. **2**

2. Raise and lower right knee. Raise left knee. Lower left knee. Hold one measure. **3**

3. Raise and lower right knee. Raise and lower left knee. Drop to right knee on ground. Stand. **4**

4. Raise and lower right knee. Raise and lower left knee. Drop to right knee. Drop to left knee. Stand. **5**

Verse:
5. Raise and lower right knee. Raise and lower left knee. Kneel on right knee. Kneel on left knee. Touch right elbow to ground. Stand. **6**

6. Raise and lower right knee. Raise and lower left knee. Kneel right. Kneel left. Touch right elbow to ground. Touch left elbow to ground. Stand. **7**

7. Raise and lower right knee. Raise and lower left knee. Kneel on right knee. Kneel on left knee. Touch right elbow to ground. Touch left elbow to ground. Touch forehead to ground, Stand. **8**

FROM UNTIL THE WHISTLE BLOWS: A COLLECTION OF GAMES, DANCES, AND ACTIVITIES FOR EIGHT- TO TWELVE-YEAR-OLDS ©1977 GOODYEAR PUBLISHING COMPANY, INC.

5

DANCE OF GREETING   DENMARK

Basic Steps: Bow, stamp, run
Records: RCA LPM 1624; Victor 45-6183, 20432; Folkraft 1187;
Russell 726
Formation: Single circle, all facing circle center.

Steps	*Measures*
1. Clap, clap, bow to partner.	**1**
2. Clap, clap, bow to neighbor.	**2**
3. Stamp right, stamp left.	**3**
4. Turn singly in 4 running steps.	**4**
Repeat steps 1-4.	**5-8**
5. All join hands and circle 16 steps to right.	**9-12**
6. Reverse and run 16 steps to left.	**13-16**

5

CHIMES OF DUNKIRK　　　　FRANCE

Basic Steps: Skip, stamp
Records: Columbia A-3016, Folkraft 1188, Victor 45-6176, 17327
Formation: Double circle, partners facing, hands on hips.

Steps	*Measures*
1. Stamp left, stamp right, stamp left, hold one count.	**1-2**
2. Clap, clap, clap.	**3-4**
3. Join both hands and circle 8 running steps.	**5-8**
4. Join inside hands and skip counterclockwise around the circle 16 skips.	**9-16**

Related Activities:
• Where is France?
• What does the language sound like?
• What is the weather like?
• Do children there play the same games you play?

5

94

FROM *UNTIL THE WHISTLE BLOWS: A COLLECTION OF GAMES, DANCES, AND ACTIVITIES FOR EIGHT- TO TWELVE-YEAR-OLDS* © 1977 GOODYEAR PUBLISHING COMPANY, INC.

THE WHEAT   CZECHOSLOVAKIA

Basic Steps: Walk, skip
Records: Victor 45-6182, RCA Victor LPM 1625
Formation: Sets of threes with hands joined, all facing counterclockwise around a circle.

Steps	*Measures*
1. Walk forward 16 bouncy steps.	**1-4**
2. Middle child hooks right elbows with child on his right. Together, they skip 8 steps in circle in place.	**5-8**
3. Middle child hooks left elbows with child on his left. Together, they skip 6 steps in circle in place.	**8-12**
4. During the last 2 skips, the middle child moves forward one set to new partners.	**12-16**

Note:
Switch positions of children in threesomes so each child has an opportunity to be in the middle.

Related Activities:
- Where is Czechoslovakia?
- What countries is it near?
- What does the country look like?
- How do you say "hello" and "good-bye" in Czech?

FROM *UNTIL THE WHISTLE BLOWS: A COLLECTION OF GAMES, DANCES, AND ACTIVITIES FOR EIGHT- TO TWELVE-YEAR-OLDS* © 1977 GOODYEAR PUBLISHING COMPANY, INC.

5

POP GOES THE WEASEL   USA

Basic Step: Skip
Records: RCA Victor LPM 1623, Columbia A-3078, Folkraft 1329,
Victor 45-6180, 20151
Formation: Sets of threes holding hands (to make small circles); all sets
arranged in a large circle; children numbered off 1, 2, 3 in
each set.

Steps	*Measures*
1. Skip 4 steps to the left.	**1-2**
2. Skip 4 steps to the right.	**3-4**
3. Balance—step in to center of little circles with right foot and touch left foot to side of right. Then step out with left foot, and touch right foot to side of left.	**5-6**
4. The child whose number (1, 2, or 3) is called becomes the weasel and ''pops'' under the arms held up by the other two children in the set, progressing counterclockwise to the next group to start all over.	**7-8**

Note:
Call out different numbers yourself
or play the record through three
times so all have a chance to be
the weasel.

FROM UNTIL THE WHISTLE BLOWS: A COLLECTION OF GAMES, DANCES, AND ACTIVITIES FOR EIGHT- TO TWELVE-YEAR-OLDS © 1977 GOODYEAR PUBLISHING COMPANY, INC.

5

EVALUATION

Area: Rhythms and Dance
Skills: Rhythm Identification
Sliding

Name _____ **Date** _____

Task	Check one or more
1. Slide to music.	Moves in time to music ☐ Does not move in time to music ☐

Additional comments:

EVALUATION

Area: Rhythms and Dance
Skills: Rhythm Identification
Sliding

Name _____ **Date** _____

Task	Check one or more
1. Slide to music.	Moves in time to music ☐ Does not move in time to music ☐

Additional comments:

BINGO USA

Basic Steps: Walk, grand right and left
Records: RCA Victor LPM 1623; Victor 45-6172, 41-6172; Folkraft
1189
Formation: Partners in single circle, girl on boy's right, all facing center.

Words	Measures	Actions
A big black dog sat on the back porch,	1-2	Walk 8 steps to the right.
And Bingo was his name.	3-4	Walk 8 steps to the left.
Repeat two lines above.	5-8	Repeat first 16 steps.
B-I-N-G-O	9-10	Walk 4 steps to the center of the circle, bringing your arms up.
B-I-N-G-O	11-12	Walk out 4 steps, lowering your arms.
B-I-N-G-O	13-14	Walk in 4 steps.
And Bingo was his name. B-I-N-G-O	15-16	Walk out 4 steps. Grand right and left—partners face each other and join right hands. Still clasping hands, they walk past each other, each giving his/her left hand to the next child he/she meets. Then right, left, right. As each passes another, a letter of "Bingo" is called. "O" is new partner. The boy puts his new partner on his right, and the dance is repeated.

Related Activities:
Talk about how to care for
animals. What are the correct ways
to handle, feed, and train them?

5

SHOEMAKER'S DANCE   DENMARK

Basic Step: Skip
Records: RCA Victor LPM 1624; Victor 20450,45-6171; Folkraft 1187; Columbia A-3038
Formation: Double circle, partners facing, hands on hips.

Steps	*Measures*
1. Revolve fists around each other 4 times to pantomine winding thread.	**1**
2. Revolve fists around each other 4 times in opposite direction.	**2**
3. Pull fists back as if breaking thread twice.	**3**
4. Tap fist to fist 3 times, as if driving nails into shoe.	**4**
Repeat steps 1-4.	**5-8**
5. Partners face counterclockwise, join inside hands, and skip 16 steps around circle. (*Variation:* Do step 4 face-to-face and back-to-back.)	**9-16**
Repeat from beginning.	

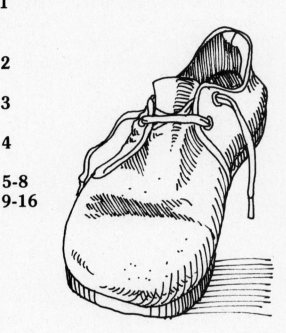

Related Activities:

- What do we call a man who makes shoes?
- How are shoes made?
- What materials are used to make shoes?
- Are there different kinds of shoes? Name some (e.g., cowboy boots, tennis shoes, ballet slippers, toe shoes, snowshoes.)
- How are they designed for the job that they do?
- What animals wear shoes? (E.g., horses.)
- What do we call the person who puts shoes on a horse? (E.g., blacksmith, farrier.)

5

FROM UNTIL THE WHISTLE BLOWS: A COLLECTION OF GAMES, DANCES, AND ACTIVITIES FOR EIGHT- TO TWELVE-YEAR-OLDS © 1977 GOODYEAR PUBLISHING COMPANY, INC.

CARROUSEL   SWEDEN

Basic Steps: Slide, stamp
Records: RCA Victor LPM 1625 or 45-6179, Folkraft 1183
Formation: Double circle, all facing center of circle; inside children join hands; outside children place hands on hips of their partner in front of them.

Steps	Measures
1. All move 14 slow slides (step-close) to the right.	**1-14**
2. Stamp 4 times in place, right-left-right-left.	**15-16**
3. Move 16 fast gallop slides to the right.	**17-24**
4. Move 12 gallop slides to the left.	**25-31**
5. Partners change places in 4 walking steps.	**32**

Repeat dance from beginning, reversing directions.

Related Activities:
- What is a carrousel?
- What is another name for a carrousel?
- Where might you find one?
- Can you draw one?
- Pretend you are a carrousel pony moving up and down in a circle.

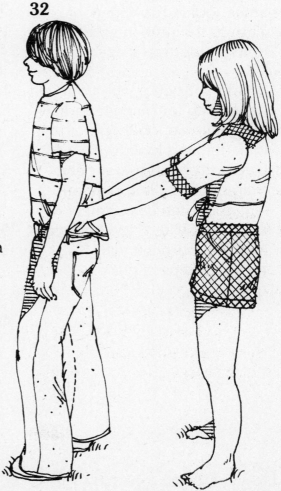

5

INDIAN RAIN DANCE   **USA**

Basic Step: Toe-heel step
Record: Folkraft F1192B
Formation: Single circle facing center, or lines or scattered formation, all facing same direction.

Steps	Measures
Part I	
1. With your arms crossed and your elbows raised, bend from the waist and bow, then return to upright position, 4 times.	**1-4**
2. Walk forward 4 steps, raising your arms to the sky, backward 4 steps, lowering your arms.	**5-8**
3. Raise your arms to the sky 4 times, looking up with your reach.	**9-12**
4. Turn to the right in small circle doing 8 toe-heel steps.	**13-16**
Part II	
1. Shade your eyes with your hand, step to the right and look, left and look, right and look, left and look.	**1-4**
2. Cup your hand to your ear. Step right and left, right and left, and listen each time.	**5-8**
3. Turn right with 8 toe-heel steps in place. Turn left with 8 toe-heel steps in place.	**9-16**

5

102

FROM *UNTIL THE WHISTLE BLOWS: A COLLECTION OF GAMES, DANCES, AND ACTIVITIES FOR EIGHT- TO TWELVE-YEAR-OLDS* © 1977 GOODYEAR PUBLISHING COMPANY, INC.

Measures

Part III

1. Jump high into air.   **1-2**
   Alternatively covering and
   uncovering your mouth with
   your hand, do an Indian call
   ("woo, woo, woo").
2. Repeat jump and call.   **3-4**
3. Walk forward 4 toe-heel steps,   **5-8**
   then backward 4 toe-heel
   steps.

Repeat steps 1-3.

4. End by raising your right hand,   **9-16**
   palm forward, and saying,
   "How."

Related Activities:

Talk about American Indians—the
great variety of their tribes,
cultures, costumes, languages,
customs, crafts, and legends.

5

Other Dances Suggested for This Level

- Did You Ever See a Lassie—*Victor 45-5066, Folkraft N83, E-Z 78 902A*
- Jolly Is the Miller—*Folkraft 1192, Victor 45-5067, American Play Party 1185*
- Shoo Fly—*Folkraft 1102 or 1185, Decca 1822*
- Ach Ja—*E-Z 906B*
- A-Hunting We Will Go—*Folkraft 1191, Victor 45-5064, 22759*
- How D'ye Do My Partner—*Victor 21685, Folkraft 1190*
- Rig a Jig Jig—*Folkraft 1199*
- Bridge of Avignon—*RCA Victor LPM 1625*
- Polly Wolly Doodle—*RCA Victor LPM 1625*
- Jingle Bells—*Folkraft 1080*

EVALUATION

Area: Rhythms and Dance
Skills: Rhythm
Coordination

Name _____ **Date** _____

Task	Check one or more
1. "Bingo" grand right and left movement.	Moves through grand right and left easily using correct hand ☐ Becomes disoriented ☐
2. Skip, slide, toe-heel step.	Generally moves in time to music ☐ Does not move in time to music ☐ Problem step: _____

Additional comments:

EVALUATION

Area: Rhythms and Dance
Skills: Rhythm
Coordination

Name _____ **Date** _____

Task	Check one or more
1. "Bingo" grand right and left movement.	Moves through grand right and left easily using correct hand ☐ Becomes disoriented ☐
2. Skip, slide, toe-heel step.	Generally moves in time to music ☐ Does not move in time to music ☐ Problem step: _____

Additional comments:

THE CRESTED HEN   DENMARK

Basic Step: Step-hop
Record: Victor 45-6176, 21619; Folkraft 1159, 1194
Formation: Sets of threes (two girls and a boy or two boys and a girl) in a circle.

Steps	*Measures*
1. Starting on right foot, take 7 step-hops to the right and jump on count 8.	**1-8**
2. Starting on left foot, take 7 step-hops to the left and jump on count 8.	**9-16**
3. Child on right moves under archway (hands joined, arms held high) formed by child in the middle and child on the left. Middle child follows under arch. All do step-hops (in place and moving).	**17-24**
4. Child on the left moves under archway (hands joined, arms held high) formed by child in the middle and child on the right. All do step-hops (in place and moving).	**25-32**

Repeat entire dance.

Related Activities:
- Discuss gender names given to animals (e.g., rooster or cock–hen, colt–filly, bull–cow, buck–doe, gander–goose, stallion–mare).
- Show pictures of animals for familiarity.

5

BLEKING   SWEDEN

Basic Step: Bleking step—Start with weight on left foot and right heel
extended forward, toe up. In a hopping motion, exchange
position of feet.
Records: RCA Victor LPM 1622; Victor 45-6169, 20989, Folkraft 1188
Formation: Double circle, partners facing, both hands joined.

Steps	*Measures*
1. Do 2 slow bleking steps (right, left) and 3 fast (right, left, right). Repeat 3 times. (Cue by calling out, "Slow, slow, quick, quick, quick.")	**1-8**
2. Do 4 step-hops in place, starting on right foot.	**9-10**
3. Passing right shoulders with partner, change places in 4 step-hops.	**11-12**
4. Repeat steps 2 and 3, returning to home position.	**13-16**

Repeat entire dance.

FROM UNTIL THE WHISTLE BLOWS: A COLLECTION OF GAMES, DANCES, AND ACTIVITIES FOR EIGHT- TO TWELVE-YEAR-OLDS © 1977 GOODYEAR PUBLISHING COMPANY, INC.

LA RASPA   MEXICO

Basic Step: Bleking step
Records: Folkraft 1190, RCA 1623, Columbia 38135, World of Fun
M106
Formation: Double circle, partners facing, hands on hips.

Steps	*Measures*
1. Do 3 bleking steps (right, left, right), hold, then do 3 more (left, right, left).	**1-4**
Repeat step 1 three times.	**5-16**
2. Hook right elbows with partner and skip in a circle.	**17-20**
3. Hook left elbows with partner and skip in a circle.	**21-24**
Repeat steps 2 and 3 (measures 17-24).	**25-32**

Related Activities:
- Where is Mexico?
- What language is spoken there? Can you count in that language? (E.g., *uno, dos, tres, . . .*)
- Can you name some foods eaten there? (E.g., *taco, guacamole, tostada, frijoles, tortillas.*)
- Can you name some articles of clothing worn there? (E.g., *bolero, huaraches, sarape, mantilla, sombrero.*)

5

KINDERPOLKA GERMANY

Basic Step: Step-close
Record: RCA Victor LPM 1625, Folkraft 1187, Victor 45-6179
Formation: Single circle, partners facing, both hands joined and extended to sides.

Steps	*Measures*
1. Moving with inside feet, do two draw steps— step and close, step and close—toward center of circle. Stamp three times.	**1-2**
2. Repeat step 1, moving in the opposite direction.	**3-4**
Repeat steps 1 and 2 (measures 1-4).	**5-8**
3. Slap own thighs, clap hands together, slap partner's hands 3 times quickly.	**9-10**
Repeat step 3.	**11-12**
4. Shake right hand with index finger extended 3 times. (Prop elbow in palm of free hand.)	**13**
5. Shake left hand with index finger extended 3 times.	**14**
6. Turn all the way around in place and stamp 3 times.	**15-16**
Repeat entire dance.	

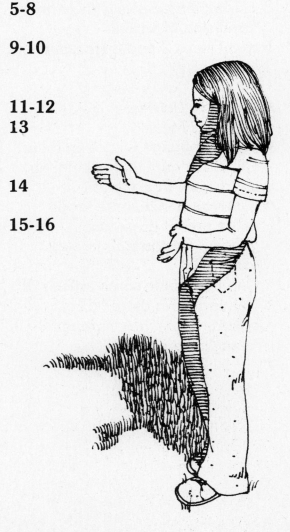

Related Activities:

- Where is Germany?
- What countries is it next to?
- What is the terrain like?
- How do you say "hello" and "good-bye" in German?

FROM UNTIL THE WHISTLE BLOWS: A COLLECTION OF GAMES, DANCES, AND ACTIVITIES FOR EIGHT- TO TWELVE-YEAR-OLDS © 1977 GOODYEAR PUBLISHING COMPANY, INC.

KOROBUSHKA   RUSSIA

Basic Steps: Schottische, balance
Records: Kismet 106, Folk Dancer MH 1059, Imperial 1022, World of Fun M108
Formation: Double circle, partners facing, inside child's back to circle center.

Steps	*Measures*

Part I

1. Do 1 schottische step away from circle center (inside child—left, right, left-hop; outside child—right, left, right-hop). **1-2**
2. Reverse and repeat step 1. **3-4**
3. Repeat step 1 (measures 1 and 2). **5-6**
4. In place, jump with feet apart, jump with feet crossed, jump with feet together. **7-8**

Part II

1. Drop hands, roll to right one turn in 3 steps and clap hands over right shoulder. **9-10**
2. Roll back to left one turn in 3 steps and clap hands over left shoulder. **11-12**
3. Balance step. (Join right hands with partner. Step forward toward partner on right foot, back in place with left foot.) **13-14**
4. Holding partner's right hand, change places with partner in walking steps. **15-16**
5. Repeat steps 1-4 (measures 1-8). **17-24**

Repeat dance from beginning.

FROM UNTIL THE WHISTLE BLOWS: A COLLECTION OF GAMES, DANCES, AND ACTIVITIES FOR EIGHT- TO TWELVE-YEAR-OLDS © 1977 GOODYEAR PUBLISHING COMPANY, INC.

COME LET US BE JOYFUL   GERMANY

Basic Steps: Walk, skip

Records: Victor 45-6177, RCA Victor LPM 1622, Folkraft 1195, World of Fun M102

Formation: Groups of threes facing each other (boy between two girls or girl between two boys); threesomes arranged like wheel spokes forming a large circle.

Steps	*Measures*
1. Starting with left foot, walk forward 3 steps. Girls curtsy, boys bow to opposite.	**1-2**
2. Starting with right, walk backward 3 steps. Girls curtsy, boys bow.	**3-4**
Repeat steps 1 and 2.	**5-8**
3. Boy hooks right elbows with girl on his right and skips 4 steps.	**9-10**
4. Boy hooks left elbows with girl on his left and skips 4 steps.	**11-12**
Repeat steps 3 and 4.	**13-16**
Repeat step 1.	**17-18**
5. Threesomes walk forward 8 steps, meshing through threesome facing them, passing left shoulders, and advancing to a new threesome.	**19-20**
Repeat entire dance.	

Related Activities:

Discuss safety and the concept of passing left shoulder to left shoulder, whether walking, riding a bike, or driving a car.

FROM UNTIL THE WHISTLE BLOWS: A COLLECTION OF GAMES, DANCES, AND ACTIVITIES FOR EIGHT- TO TWELVE-YEAR-OLDS © 1977 GOODYEAR PUBLISHING COMPANY, INC.

Other Dances Suggested for This Level

- Paw Paw Patch—*E-Z 2003B, Folkraft 1189*
- Three Blind Mice—Children sing own accompaniment
- Jump Jim Jo—*RCA Victor LPM 1625*
- Hansel and Gretel—*Victor 45-6182*
- Chesborgar—*Victor 45-6182, RCA Victor LPM 1624, Folkraft 1196*
- Gustaf's Skoul—*Victor 45-6170, RCA Victor LPM 1622, Folkraft 1175*
- Bummel Schottische—*RCA Victor LPM 1622*
- Nixie Polka—*RCA Victor LPM 1625*

EVALUATION

Area: Rhythms and Dance
Skills: Rhythm
　　　　　Specific Steps

Name _____ **Date** _____

Task	Check one or more
1. Step-hop, bleking, step-close, schottische steps.	Performs in rhythm ☐ Cannot perform in rhythm ☐
2. Change directions.	Displays control, changes directions easily ☐ Cannot change directions easily ☐
	Problem step: _____

Additional comments:

EVALUATION

Area: Rhythms and Dance
Skills: Rhythm
　　　　　Specific Steps

Name _____ **Date** _____

Task	Check one or more
1. Step-hop, bleking, step-close, schottische steps.	Performs in rhythm ☐ Cannot perform in rhythm ☐
2. Change directions.	Displays control, changes directions easily ☐ Cannot change directions easily ☐
	Problem step: _____

Additional comments:

FROM *UNTIL THE WHISTLE BLOWS: A COLLECTION OF GAMES, DANCES, AND ACTIVITIES FOR FOUR- TO EIGHT-YEAR-OLDS*
© 1976 GOODYEAR PUBLISHING COMPANY, INC.

Record Sources

1. Eastern United States

Dance Record Center
1161 Broad Street
Newark, N.J. 07714

David McKay, Inc.
750 Third Avenue
New York, N.Y. 10017

Educational Activities, Inc.
P.O. Box 392
Freeport, N.Y. 11520

Educational Record Sales
157 Chambers Street
New York, N.Y. 10007

Folkraft Records
1159 Broad Street
Newark, N.J. 07714

Hoctor Educational Records, Inc.
Waldwick, N.J. 97463

Kimbo Educational Records
P.O. Box 246
Deal, N.J. 07723

Folk Dance House
108 W. 16th Street
New York, N.Y. 10011

Selva & Sons, Inc.
1607 Broadway
New York, N.Y. 10019

RCA Victor Education Department J
1133 Avenue of the Americas
New York, N.Y. 10036

2. Midwestern United States

Leo's Advance Theatrical Company
2451 N. Sacramento Avenue
Chicago, Ill. 60647

Loshin's
215 E. 8th Street
Cincinnati, Ohio 45202

Rhythm Record Company
9203 Nichols Road
Oklahoma City, Okla. 73120

3. Southern/Southwestern United States

Record Center
2581 Piedmont Road N.E.
Atlanta, Ga. 30324

Merrback Records Service
P.O. Box 7308
Houston, Texas 77000

Cross Trail Square Dance Center
4150 S. W. 70th Court
Miami, Fla. 33155

4. Western United States

Rhythms Productions Records
Department J, Box 34485
Los Angeles, Calif. 90034

Russell Records
P.O. Box 3318
Ventura, Calif. 93003

Square Dance Square
P.O. Box 689
Santa Barbara, Calif. 93100

Standard Records & Hi Fi Company
1028 N. E. 65th
Seattle, Wash. 98115

Children's Music Center
5373 W. Pico Blvd.
Los Angeles, Calif. 90019

Bowmar Records
4563 Colorado Blvd.
Los Angeles, Calif. 90039

Decker's Records
12425 Trent
Spokane, Wash. 99216

Master Record Service
708 East Garfield
Phoenix, Ariz. 85000

5. Canada

Canadian F.D.S. Educational Recordings
605 King Street
W. Toronto, 2B, Canada

5

STUNTS
AND
TUMBLING

6.

This chapter covers the exploration of basic movement skills, imitative movements, and simple stunts. The activities have been selected for four- to eight-year-old children. They require relatively small working areas and the following few items of equipment:

- balls (small, tennis type)
- beanbags
- books (light)
- chalk
- masking tape
- mats or thick blankets (folded)

For children aged four through seven, the emphasis should be on exploring, experimenting, acquiring, and adapting a wide variety of skills as they learn the fundamentals of jumping, landing, supporting and shifting weight, curling, rolling, and body extension.

With children eight years old and older, more attention should be given to the development of control and balance, the coordination of movements, and the ability to perform these movements in patterns or set sequences.

This chapter is divided into four sections. Each section begins with a list of warm-up activities. One or more of these should precede each skills learning session. Following each set of activities is an evaluation sheet for use in assessing skill attainment.

While stunts and tumbling activities generally involve familiar movements, the skill itself may be new in both nature and physical orientation; therefore, children will not naturally progress from one stunt to another without good instruction and demonstration. When first introduced, activities should be presented simply and briefly. Tips on how to dress up a skill should be added later. Because children learn stunts and tumbling activities more by imitation than by verbal instruction, you should be prepared to demonstrate the activity, then let *everyone* try it. You might ask children who catch on quickly to provide additional demonstration as needed.

In stunts and tumbling activities, safety must be a prime consideration. Accidents are most likely to happen when children are pushed too quickly from one activity to another or when inadequate instruction is given. The best insurance against mishaps is provided by good instruction, constant supervision, proper spotting, and sufficient skill practice.

Though activities are presented only once, they should be repeated several times so that individual skills can be mastered and perfected.

Consideration should be given to clothing. Pants or shorts, tennis shoes and socks, and comfortable shirts or tops allow children to move easily.

During instruction and performance, students should be arranged so that they can see and hear well and move safely. Suggested formations are

1. Well-spaced Lines

2. Free Formation

3. Semicircle

Possible mat arrangements include

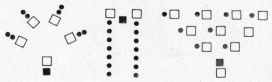

WARM-UP ACTIVITIES (for pages 118-133)

1. CAN YOU REACH? CAN YOU TOUCH?
Standing in well-spaced lines,
- how high can you reach, jump?
- can you touch your elbows to your knees, your ears to your shoulders?

Sitting in well-spaced lines,
- can you touch your elbows to the ground, your knees to your chest?
- can you touch your nose to your toes, your hands to your toes?

2. RUN AND WALK IN PLACE
Standing in a well-spaced formation, walk and run in place swinging your arms, varying your speed, and lifting your knees to your chest.

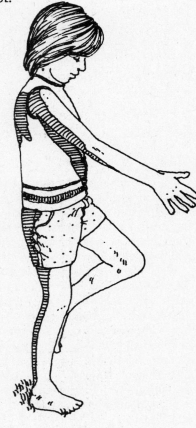

3. WATCH ME FLY
Standing in a well-spaced line or lines, follow the leader, taking short, running steps in a curving pattern, arms extended. Dip your arms as you turn. Vary your height (altitude): run on tiptoes to go over mountains; bend your knees to go through the valley.

FROM UNTIL THE WHISTLE BLOWS: A COLLECTION OF GAMES, DANCES, AND ACTIVITIES FOR EIGHT- TO TWELVE-YEAR-OLDS © 1977 GOODYEAR PUBLISHING COMPANY, INC.

6

FROM UNTIL THE WHISTLE BLOWS: A COLLECTION OF GAMES, DANCES, AND ACTIVITIES FOR EIGHT- TO TWELVE-YEAR-OLDS ©1977 GOODYEAR PUBLISHING COMPANY, INC.

4.   SHAKE, RATTLE, AND ROLL

Standing in a well-spaced line or circle, follow the leader in

- shaking your right hand, elbow circle first then the whole arm (repeat on left side);
- shaking your right foot, your whole leg (repeat on left side);
- making circles with your hips, head, trunk;
- shaking all over.

5.   FLOPSY MOPSY DOLL

Standing well spaced in free formation, move like a rag doll, very relaxed, swinging your head, body, and arms.

6.   SIMON SAYS

Standing well spaced in free formation, children are cued to

- touch their toes, knees, waist;
- touch their hands overhead;
- bend forward, backward;
- touch their hands behind their head, their waist, their knees.

To make the exercise more difficult, designate a specific hand, foot, etc. (e.g., right hand to right foot).

7.   DIRECTIONAL CUES

Standing well spaced in free formation and watching out for others, walk, hop, jump, and run forward, backward, sideways, and in place, as cued.

6

ONE-LEG BALANCE   10 MIN.

Purpose: Development of coordination and balance
Equipment: 1 beanbag or 1 small, light book per child
Play Area: Any clean, flat area

Directions:

Standing in well-spaced lines, lift one foot and extend your arms to the sides for balance.

- See how long you can hold this position "very still."
- Vary the position of your arms (put them on your head, your hips, fold them across your chest), or balance a beanbag or book on your head, shoulder, or hand.

Now try these activities while standing on the opposite foot.

FROM *UNTIL THE WHISTLE BLOWS: A COLLECTION OF GAMES, DANCES, AND ACTIVITIES FOR EIGHT- TO TWELVE-YEAR-OLDS* © 1977 GOODYEAR PUBLISHING COMPANY, INC.

TIGHTROPE WALK

10 MIN.

Purpose: Development of coordination and balance
Equipment: 1 beanbag or 1 small, light book per child
Play Area: Any clean, flat area where lines are painted or can be drawn with chalk

Directions:

On a line painted or drawn on the floor or ground,
- walk normally, holding your arms out for balance as you pretend to be a tightrope walker.
- walk varying the position of your arms.
- walk heel-to-toe.
- hop.

Related Activities:

- Talk about a circus: What kinds of animals do you see there? What do the different performers do?
- Plan and stage a "circus" to demonstrate the skills you have acquired.

BOUNCING BALL   10 MIN.

Purpose: General conditioning, balance, landing properly
Equipment: 1 ball for demonstration
Play Area: Clean, flat, smooth area in classroom, gym, or yard
Formation: Free, well spaced.

Directions:
- Bounce a utility ball vigorously and let the children watch the height of the bounce taper off.
- Have children imitate a bouncing ball starting from a bent knee position, keeping their backs straight. Instruct them to vary the height of their "bounce" as cued. Watch that they land first on their toes, distributing their weight over the arch and then to the heel. Teach them to absorb the shock of landing by letting their knees give (bend) slightly.

Related Activities:
Talk about the concept of "bouncing." What makes a ball bounce? Why do some balls bounce higher than others? Why does the height (vigor) of the bounce deteriorate? What is *gravity*?

6

FROM *UNTIL THE WHISTLE BLOWS: A COLLECTION OF GAMES, DANCES, AND ACTIVITIES FOR EIGHT- TO TWELVE-YEAR-OLDS* © 1977 GOODYEAR PUBLISHING COMPANY, INC.

FOREHEAD TOUCH

5 MIN.

Purpose: General conditioning, balance
Equipment: Mats
Play Area: Clean, flat, smooth area in classroom, gym, or yard
Formation: Well-spaced lines or free formation.

Directions:

- Kneel on both knees with your feet pointed to the rear and your arms extended to the rear for balance.
- Lean forward slowly, touch your forehead to the mat, then return to your original position.
- Try it again, varying the position of your arms.

6

ELEVATOR   5 MIN.

Purpose: General conditioning, balance
Equipment: None
Play Area: Clean, flat, smooth area in classroom, gym, or yard
Formation: Well-spaced lines or free formation.

Directions:
With your arms out and your back straight, pretend to be an elevator moving slowly up and down by bending your knees.

Related Activities:
- Look up the word *elevator*. What does it mean? (I.e., "one that raises or lifts up anything.") What does an elevator do?
- What other devices are used to raise and lower things?
- What other things go up and down?

6

ROCKER

10 MIN.

Purpose: Development of balance, gross muscle coordination
Equipment: Mats or thick blankets (folded)
Play Area: Classroom (cleared) or gym
Formation: Semicircle of mats; children standing on mats facing you.

Directions:
- Assume a crouched position with your weight on your toes and your hands on the floor for balance.
- Roll backward, clasping your hands around your knees.
- Rock rhythmically forward and backward.

Related Activities:
Talk about the concept of "rocking." Name some things that rock (e.g., a boat on water, a rocker or rocking chair, a hobbyhorse or rocking horse).

6

DOUBLE KNEE BALANCE   10 MIN.

Purpose: Development of balance, gross muscle coordination
Equipment: Mats or thick blankets (folded)
Play Area: Classroom (cleared) or gym
Formation: Semicircle of mats; children kneeling on mats on both knees with legs parallel, feet to rear, and body erect from the knees up.

Directions:

- Hold your right foot off the floor with your right hand, extending your left arm to the side for balance.
- Hold your left foot off the floor with your left hand, extending your right arm to the side for balance.
- With both arms extended, lift both feet off the mat and hold.
- Try it again, extending the time of your "hold."

6

FROM *UNTIL THE WHISTLE BLOWS: A COLLECTION OF GAMES, DANCES, AND ACTIVITIES FOR EIGHT- TO TWELVE-YEAR-OLDS* © 1977 GOODYEAR PUBLISHING COMPANY, INC.

GET UP

5 MIN.

Purpose: Development of balance, gross muscle coordination
Equipment: Mats or thick blankets (folded)
Play Area: Classroom (cleared) or gym
Formation: Semicircle of mats; children standing on mats facing you.

Directions:

- Fold your arms across your chest, cross your feet, and sit down slowly and smoothly without moving your arms or feet.
- Leaving your arms and feet in the same position, stand up slowly.

KANGAROO JUMP   5 MIN.

Purpose: General conditioning, flexibility, strength
Equipment: Beanbags or small balls
Play Area: Classroom, gym, or yard
Formation: Free formation in a defined area; watch out for others.

Directions:

- Place a beanbag or small ball between your knees.
- Hold your arms up close to your chest with your elbows bent and your palms facing forward.
- Move about in various directions using small jumps without dropping the beanbag or ball.

Related Activities:

- Talk about kangaroos: Where do they live? What color are they? What do they eat? What is a male kangaroo called? What is a female kangaroo called? What is a baby kangaroo called? How big is it at birth? Where does its mother carry it? What is a *marsupial*?
- Read a story about kangaroos. Consider
  Emmy Payne, *Katy No-Pocket* (Houghton Mifflin, 1944).
  Charlotte Steiner, *I'd Rather Stay With You* (Seabury, 1965).
- Write and act out a story or play about kangaroos and other animals.

6

FROM *UNTIL THE WHISTLE BLOWS: A COLLECTION OF GAMES, DANCES, AND ACTIVITIES FOR EIGHT- TO TWELVE-YEAR-OLDS* © 1977 GOODYEAR PUBLISHING COMPANY, INC.

ELEPHANT SWAY 5 MIN.

Purpose: General conditioning, flexibility
Equipment: None
Play Area: Classroom, gym, yard
Formation: Free formation in a defined area; watch out for others.

Directions:
- Bend forward from the waist, keeping your knees stiff and your arms straight, and clasping your hands to form a trunk.
- Now walk slowly, swinging your "trunk" from side to side.
- Swing your trunk low to touch your ankles.
- Lift your trunk high in the air to spray water.

Related Activities:
- Talk about elephants: Where do they live? What color are they? What do they eat? What is a male elephant called? What is a female elephant called? What is a baby elephant called? How much does it weigh at birth? What is a *pachyderm*?
- Read a story about elephants. Consider
  Jean de Brunhoff, *The Story of Babar, The Little Elephant* (Random House, 1933).
  Kathryn and Byron Jackson, *The Saggy Baggy Elephant* (Golden Press, 1947).
  Patricia Thomas, *"Stand Back,"* *Said The Elephant, "I'm, Going to Sneeze"* (Lothrop, Lee & Shepard, 1971).
- Write and act out a story about elephants and other animals—or feature them in your "circus."

6

GIRAFFE WALK

5 MIN.

Purpose: General conditioning, flexibility
Equipment: None
Play Area: Classroom, gym, yard
Formation: Free formation in a defined area; watch out for others.

Directions:

- Form the long neck of a giraffe by extending your arms straight up alongside your ears and hooking your thumbs over your head.
- Bend your hands at the wrist so that they point forward to make the giraffe's head.
- Keeping your knees stiff, move in various directions on your tiptoes.
- Stop and bend slowly forward to take a drink of water.

Related Activities:

- Talk about giraffes: Where do they live? What color are they? What is *camouflage*? What do giraffes eat? How does a giraffe's long neck help him get his dinner?
- Write and act out a story or play about giraffes and other animals. The African grasslands (veld), a circus, or a zoo might make a good setting.

FROM UNTIL THE WHISTLE BLOWS: A COLLECTION OF GAMES, DANCES, AND ACTIVITIES FOR EIGHT- TO TWELVE-YEAR-OLDS © 1977 GOODYEAR PUBLISHING COMPANY, INC.

6

SIDE ROLL

15 MIN.

Purpose: Developing flexibility and lead-up skills for rolls
Equipment: Mats or thick blankets (folded)
Play Area: Cleared classroom or gym, clean surface
Formation: Mats arranged in one or two lines; children on hands and knees on mats.

Directions:

- Decide which side (right or left) to roll toward.
- Tuck both the elbow and the knee on that side under and roll to the selected side, the back, the other side, and to your original position.
- Repeat, rolling to the other side.

6

CROCODILE CRAWL

10 MIN.

Purpose: Developing flexibility, exploring movement
Equipment: Mats or thick blankets (folded)
Play Area: Cleared classroom or gym, clean surface
Formation: Children lying face down well spaced on the floor or ground; all moving in the same direction.

Directions:

- Bend your arms.
- Move along the floor or ground by advancing the same hand and foot to start, then the opposite hand and foot.
- Turn over on your back and try to move in the same way, with your hands bent down and placed alongside you.

Related Activities:

- Talk about crocodiles: Where do they live? What do they look like? Name some other animals, real or imaginary, living or extinct, that resemble the crocodile. (E.g., lizard, dragon, alligator, dinosaur.) What is a *reptile*?

- Read a story about crocodiles. Consider
Bernard Waber, *The House on East 88th Street* (Houghton Mifflin, 1962).
Bernard Waber, *Lyle, Lyle, Crocodile* (Houghton Mifflin, 1965).
Bernard Waber, *Lyle and the Birthday Party* (Houghton Mifflin, 1966).
Bernard Waber, *Lovable Lyle* (Houghton Mifflin, 1969).

6

FROM *UNTIL THE WHISTLE BLOWS: A COLLECTION OF GAMES, DANCES, AND ACTIVITIES FOR EIGHT- TO TWELVE-YEAR-OLDS* © 1977 GOODYEAR PUBLISHING COMPANY, INC.

BEAR WALK

5 MIN.

Purpose: Developing basic movement skills, flexibility, endurance, and strength

Equipment: None

Play Area: Clean, flat, smooth surface in a classroom, gym, or grassy yard

Formation: Well spaced; all moving in the same direction.

Directions:

- Put your hands and feet flat on the floor, rounding your back and keeping your arms and legs straight.
- Walk slowly, rolling from side to side. Move your right arm then your right foot. Move your left arm, then your left foot.

Related Activities:

- Talk about bears: Where do they live? What do they eat? What sound do they make? What are baby bears called? Can you name several kinds of bears? (E.g., grizzly bear, polar bear, teddy bear.) Is a panda a bear? What about a koala? Why is a teddy bear called a *teddy* bear?

- Read a story about bears. Consider
  Michael Bond, *A Bear Called Paddington* (Dell Yearling Book, 1974).
  Don Freeman, *Corduroy* (Viking Press, 1968).
  A. A. Milne, *The Pooh Story Book* (E. P. Dutton, 1954).
  Liesel Moak Skorpen, *Charles* (Harper & Row, 1971).

6

RABBIT JUMP   5 MIN.

Purpose: Developing basic movement skills, flexibility, endurance, and strength

Equipment: None

Play Area: Clean, flat, smooth surface in a classroom, gym, or grassy yard

Formation: Well-spaced; all moving in the same direction.

Directions:

- Assume a squat position.
- Move your arms forward together, and put your weight on them.
- "Jump" your feet forward so that they are between your arms.

Related Activities:

- Talk about rabbits: Where do they live? What do they eat? What sound do they make? Can you wiggle your nose like a rabbit?

- Read a story about rabbits. Consider

  Du Bose Heyward, *The Country Bunny and the Little Gold Shoes* (Houghton Mifflin, 1939).

  Robert Kraus, *The Bunny's Nutshell Library* (Harper & Row, 1965).

  Robert Kraus, *Daddy Long Ears* (Windmill, 1970).

  Beatrix Potter, *The Tale of Peter Rabbit* (Frederick Warne, 1904).

6

FROM UNTIL THE WHISTLE BLOWS: A COLLECTION OF GAMES, DANCES, AND ACTIVITIES FOR EIGHT- TO TWELVE-YEAR-OLDS © 1977 GOODYEAR PUBLISHING COMPANY, INC.

CAMEL WALK   5 MIN.

Purpose: Developing basic movement skills, flexibility, endurance, and strength
Equipment: None
Play Area: Clean, flat, smooth surface in a classroom, gym, or grassy yard
Formation: Well-spaced free formation; all moving in the same direction.

Directions:

- Cross your arms behind your back and hold opposite elbows.
- Bend forward at the waist, keeping your head up and your eyes straight ahead.
- Walk slowly, lifting your heels up behind following each step.

Related Activities:

Talk about camels: Where do they live? What do they eat? What do they use their hump for? What is the difference between a *Bactrian camel* and a *dromedary*? Do camels *ruminate*?

6

EVALUATION

Area: Stunts and Tumbling
Skills: Balance
Lead-up Skills

Name _____   **Date** _____

Task	Check one or more
1. One-Leg Balance Balance on one leg with your arms extended at shoulder height. Repeat on opposite foot. Hold each position for a count of 5.	Can distinguish right from left as directed ☐ Can hold position still ☐ Uses arms and leg held up to keep balance ☐
2. Tightrope Walk With your arms extended at shoulder height for balance, walk on a painted or drawn line 3 to 4 feet long, keeping your eyes straight ahead.	Walks without watching ground ☐ Uses arms effectively to maintain balance ☐
3. Elevator Holding your arms out, bend your knees as the elevator descends. When in a deep crouch position, straighten up slowly. Keep your back straight.	Descends in a slow, controlled manner ☐ Ascends in a slow, controlled manner ☐
4. Side Roll On mat on your hands and knees, tuck your left (right) hip and shoulder and roll to your left (right) side, to your back, to your right (left) side, and back to your starting position. Move as directed either to the right or the left, then in the opposite direction.	Rolls as directed to right or left ☐ Uses momentum to complete roll ☐ Rolls with ease to right side and to left ☐

Additional comments:

FROM *UNTIL THE WHISTLE BLOWS: A COLLECTION OF GAMES, DANCES, AND ACTIVITIES FOR EIGHT- TO TWELVE-YEAR-OLDS* © 1977 GOODYEAR PUBLISHING COMPANY, INC.

6

WARM-UP ACTIVITIES (for pages 138-152)

1. JUMPING JACKS

- Stand with your feet together and your arms straight down at your sides.
- Jump to a straddle position (feet spread shoulder width), clapping your hands over your head.
- Jump a second time, bringing your feet back together and clapping your hands in front of your body.

Continue doing this two-count exercise: apart (clap), together (clap).

2. FLOOR TO FEET

- Lie on your back with your arms folded across your chest.
- Rise to a standing position without using your arms.

Vary the exercise by changing the specified position of the hands (on head, on hips) and legs (spread slightly apart).

6

WARM-UP ACTIVITIES (continued)

3. JUMP AND CLAP
- Jump up in the air and clap your hands over your head once before you land.
- Jump again, but this time try to clap twice before you land.
- Jump again and see how many times you can clap while you are still in the air.

4. FOLLOW THE LEADER
Be the leader yourself or choose one. Other children line up behind the leader and follow him as he moves in a twisting and turning fashion, first taking short steps, then long; running, hopping, or jumping; walking on tiptoes or with knees bent; swinging his arms to accentuate long steps or big movements.

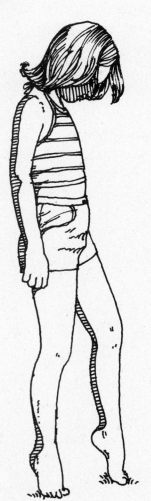

FROM UNTIL THE WHISTLE BLOWS: A COLLECTION OF GAMES, DANCES, AND ACTIVITIES FOR EIGHT- TO TWELVE-YEAR-OLDS © 1977 GOODYEAR PUBLISHING COMPANY, INC.

6

5.   SPINNING TOP

- Without losing your balance, jump into the air and make a quarter turn, landing where you are now but facing the _____ (name an object).
- Without losing your balance, jump into the air and turn half way around, landing where you are now.
- Jump into the air and turn yourself all the way around, landing where you are now.

If "quarter turn" and "turn half way around" are confusing at first, direct children to turn to face some object (red door, windows, large tree, chalkboard). To make the exercise more challenging, vary the directions ("Make a quarter turn to the *left*." "Turn half way around to the *right*.").

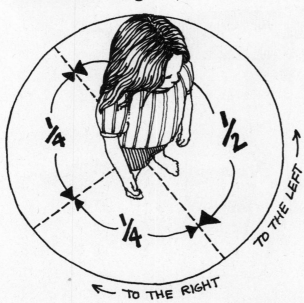

6.   HIGH KICK

- Raise your right hand to a height half way between your knee and your waist and kick your right leg to that height.
- Raise your left hand to a height half way between your knee and your waist and kick your left leg to that height.
- Continue the exercise, raising your hand and the height of your kick.
- Try the same exercise, kicking left leg to right hand and right leg to left hand.

6

CRANE DIVE   5 MIN.

Purpose: Developing balance, flexibility
Equipment: None
Play Area: Clean, flat, smooth surface in a classroom, gym, or yard
Formation: Well-spaced lines.

Directions:

- With your weight on one foot and your arms extended back along your torso for balance, lift the other leg backward.
- Keeping both legs as straight as possible and your eyes forward, slowly lean forward as far as you can without losing your balance.
- Vary the position of your arms, or see if you can pick up a small object off the floor.

FROM UNTIL THE WHISTLE BLOWS: A COLLECTION OF GAMES, DANCES, AND ACTIVITIES FOR EIGHT- TO TWELVE-YEAR-OLDS © 1977 GOODYEAR PUBLISHING COMPANY, INC.

6

STOOP AND STRETCH

10 MIN.

Purpose: Developing balance, flexibility
Equipment: Chalk, masking tape, or markers of some sort
Play Area: Clean, flat, smooth surface in a classroom, gym, or yard
Formation: Well-spaced lines or a circle with heels touching a painted or drawn line.

Directions:

- Squat down with your feet apart.
- Now see how far back through your legs you can reach without losing your balance. Have someone mark your reach point with chalk.
- See how far around and through your legs you can reach. Have someone mark your reach point.

6

INCHWORM

5 MIN.

Purpose: Developing balance, flexibility
Equipment: None
Play Area: Clean, flat, smooth surface in a classroom, gym, or yard
Formation: Well-spaced lines or free formation; all moving in the same direction.

Directions:

- Get down on all fours, putting your weight evenly on your hands and feet.
- With your back arched and your elbows and knees straight, walk your hands forward until your back is straight.
- Now walk your feet forward until they are as close to your hands as you can bring them *without* bending your knees and/or elbows.
- Vary the activity by moving one hand, one foot, then the other hand, other foot.

Related Activities:

- What is an inchworm? What does it look like? Where might you find one? What does it eat?
- What is an *inch*? A *foot*? A *yard*?

FROM UNTIL THE WHISTLE BLOWS: A COLLECTION OF GAMES, DANCES, AND ACTIVITIES FOR EIGHT- TO TWELVE-YEAR-OLDS © 1977 GOODYEAR PUBLISHING COMPANY, INC.

6

FROG JUMP

5 MIN.

Purpose: Developing basic movement skills, general conditioning
Equipment: None
Play Area: Clean, flat, smooth surface in a classroom, gym, or yard
Formation: Well-spaced lines or free formation; all moving in the same direction.

Directions:
- Squat down with your feet apart.
- Move forward by transferring your weight to your hands (arms straight), then jumping your feet forward so that your bent knees are outside your arms.
- Vary the activity by springing up and down in place or moving in a circle.

PUPPY RUN

5 MIN.

Purpose: Developing basic movement skills, general conditioning
Equipment: None
Play Area: Clean, flat, smooth surface in a classroom, gym, or yard
Formation: Well-spaced free formation; all moving in the same direction.

Directions:

- Get down on all fours, putting your weight evenly on your hands and feet and bending your knees and elbows slightly.
- With your eyes forward, walk, (run, scamper) like a happy puppy.
- Now move and bark like a happy puppy.
- Vary the activity by moving like a lame dog (holding one leg off the ground) or like a cat (moving more slowly and stretching).

Related Activities:

- What kinds of animals make good pets?
- How do you handle a dog or cat?
- How do you care for a pet?

FROM UNTIL THE WHISTLE BLOWS: A COLLECTION OF GAMES, DANCES, AND ACTIVITIES FOR EIGHT- TO TWELVE-YEAR-OLDS © 1977 GOODYEAR PUBLISHING COMPANY, INC.

6

CRICKET HOP   5 MIN.

Purpose: Developing basic movement skills, general conditioning
Equipment: None
Play Area: Clean, flat, smooth surface in a classroom, gym, or yard
Formation: Well-spaced free formation; all moving in the same direction.

Directions:

- Squat down with your feet apart.
- Holding your ankles with your hands, jump in various directions.
- Vary the height and distance of your jumps.

Related Activities:

- Talk about crickets: What color are they? What sound do they make and how do they make it? Where do they live? What do they eat?

- Read a story about a cricket. Consider

Carlo Collodi, *The Adventures of Pinocchio*, translated from the Italian by Carol Della Chiesa (Macmillan, 1925; reissued in 1969).

Felice Holman, *The Cricket Winter* (Norton, 1967).

Barbara Reid, *Carlo's Cricket* (McGraw-Hill, 1967).

George Selden, *The Cricket in Times Square* (Farrar, 1960).

6

LOG ROLL

10 MIN.

Purpose: General conditioning, developing balance and endurance
Equipment: 2 or 3 mats or several thick blankets (folded)
Play Area: Classroom (cleared), gym, or yard
Formation: Place mats or blankets end-to-end; have children line up at one end of the mats (blankets).

Directions:
- Lie down across one end of the mats with your arms extended (elbows straight) over your head, palms touching.
- Keeping your body straight, roll side over side to the other end of the mat.
- Return to the end of the line for a second turn.

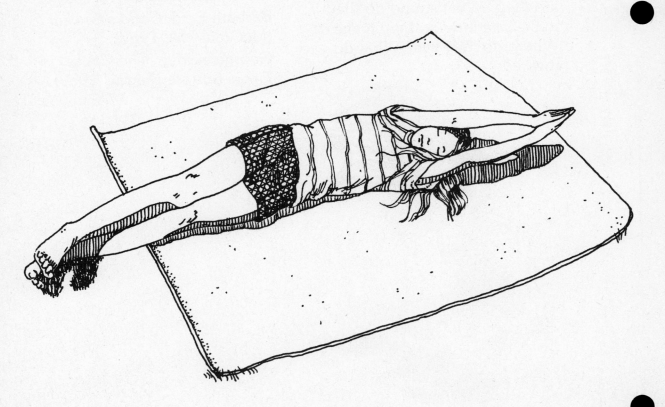

6

FROM UNTIL THE WHISTLE BLOWS: A COLLECTION OF GAMES, DANCES, AND ACTIVITIES FOR EIGHT- TO TWELVE-YEAR-OLDS © 1977 GOODYEAR PUBLISHING COMPANY, INC.

UP AND OVER 10 MIN.

Purpose: General conditioning, developing balance and endurance
Equipment: 1 mat or thick blanket (folded) for each child
Play Area: Classroom (cleared), gym, or yard
Formation: Children well-spaced, lying on mats, all facing one direction.

Directions:

- Put your arms straight along your sides, palms to the mat, to push and use for balance.
- Keeping your knees straight, raise your legs together slowly, and touch your toes to the mat above your head. (To do this activity properly, you will have to lift your back off the mat, transferring your weight to your neck, shoulders, and arms.)
- Slowly return to your starting position.
- Repeat to an even count.

6

BICYCLING   5 MIN.

Purpose: General conditioning, developing balance and endurance
Equipment: 1 mat or thick blanket (folded) for each child
Play Area: Classroom (cleared), gym, or yard
Formation: Children well spaced, lying on mats with arms at sides; all facing one direction.

Directions:
- Raise your legs and body to a vertical position so that your weight is supported on your neck, shoulders, and arms.
- Bend your arms up at the elbows and rest your hips in your hands.
- Bend your knees, and rotate your legs as if you were pedaling a bicycle.
- Vary your speed: pedal faster, slower; push hard as if you were climbing a steep hill.

Related Activities:
- Talk about bike safety. Include a demonstration of correct hand signals.
- Stage a "bicycle rodeo" in which bicycles are inspected for safety features (headlamp, horn, reflectors), bicycle owners are tested for their knowledge of traffic laws as they apply to riding a bicycle, and cyclists ride over a course designed so that they must demonstrate their ability to handle the cycle and their knowledge and use of hand signals.

6

FROM UNTIL THE WHISTLE BLOWS: A COLLECTION OF GAMES, DANCES, AND ACTIVITIES FOR EIGHT- TO TWELVE-YEAR-OLDS © 1977 GOODYEAR PUBLISHING COMPANY, INC.

ROOSTER HOP

10 MIN.

Purpose: General conditioning, developing balance, awareness of proper landing technique

Equipment: None

Play Area: Clean, flat, smooth surface in classroom, gym, or yard

Formation: Standing in well-spaced lines; all facing one direction.

Directions:

- Reaching across in back of you, grasp your left foot with your right hand and hop forward, then backward.
- Again reaching across in back of you, grasp your right foot with your left hand and hop forward, then backward.
- Watch the way you land. Let your knee give (bend) a little to absorb the shock.

Related Activities:

Hold a rooster hop race.

6

TREADMILL

5 MIN.

Purpose: General conditioning
Equipment: None
Play Area: Clean, flat, smooth surface in a classroom, gym, or yard
Formation: Well-spaced lines or free formation, all facing one direction.

Directions:

- Bend your knees to assume a squat position.
- Lean forward and place your hands flat on the floor or ground in front of your shoulders.
- Extend your left leg straight out behind you, placing the sole of your left foot on the floor or ground.
- Rocking slightly forward to place your weight temporarily on your arms, exchange the positions of your legs (draw up the left, extend the right) with a jumping motion.
- Repeat the exercise rhythmically to a count or music.

FROM UNTIL THE WHISTLE BLOWS: A COLLECTION OF GAMES, DANCES, AND ACTIVITIES FOR EIGHT- TO TWELVE-YEAR-OLDS © 1977 GOODYEAR PUBLISHING COMPANY, INC.

6

WRING THE DISHRAG   5 MIN.

Purpose: General conditioning, developing the ability to work with a partner

Equipment: None

Play Area: Clean, flat, smooth surface in a classroom, gym, or yard

Formation: Partners stand holding hands and facing each other. If your children are familiar with some basic dance formations and terms, it may be easier to give the directions for this activity if the children are in a single circle with partners facing.

Directions:

- Holding hands, raise your inside (pair nearest circle center) arms.
- Continuing to clasp both pairs of hands, turn to face the center of the circle and go under your raised arms so that your backs are together.
- Lowering that pair of arms and raising what are now the inside arms, complete your turn and end in your original position (single circle, partners facing).
- Repeat, turning in the opposite direction, that is, raising and going under outside (pair farthest from circle center) arms.

6

THREAD THE NEEDLE   5 MIN.

Purpose: General conditioning, developing flexibility and balance
Equipment: None
Play Area: Clean, flat, smooth surface in a classroom (cleared), gym, or yard
Formation: Standing in well-spaced line, circle, or free formation.

Directions:

- Interlock your fingers, palms up.
- Bend forward and step over your clasped hands with one leg, then with the other leg, ending with your hands, still clasped, behind you.
- Reverse, stepping back over your hands.
- Repeat the activity, starting with the opposite foot.

FROM UNTIL THE WHISTLE BLOWS: A COLLECTION OF GAMES, DANCES, AND ACTIVITIES FOR EIGHT- TO TWELVE-YEAR-OLDS © 1977 GOODYEAR PUBLISHING COMPANY, INC.

6

FORWARD ROLL   15 MIN.

Purpose: General conditioning, developing flexibility and balance
Equipment: Mats or thick blankets (folded)
Play Area: Clean, flat, smooth surface in a classroom (cleared), gym, or yard
Formation: Children in lines facing mats (2 or 3) placed end-to-end. Be prepared to spot each child during his first few attempts to do this activity.

Directions:
- With your feet apart, squat down and place your hands flat on the mat.
- Tuck your head between your knees.
- Springing slightly to transfer your weight from your feet to your hands, roll forward in a tuck position.
- As your weight is transferred from your hands to the nape of your neck and then your back, bring your hands forward to clasp your shins.
- Continue rolling until your feet are under you, then stand.
- Vary by doing continuous rolls (do not stand in between) or by rolling with your legs crossed.

Note:
The nape of neck, not the head, should touch the mat first. If a child is rolling over one shoulder, suggest he spread his feet farther apart, distribute his weight evenly on both, and push off equally with both.

To Spot:
"Lift" and push in direction of roll at the nape of the neck and at the shin.

Related Activities:
- Talk about things that roll easily. What shape are they? (E.g., curved, round.) Will you roll more easily if you bend (curve) your back or keep it straight?
- Talk about the adaptability of the human body to various positions. What shapes can you make with your body?

See illustration on page 152.

FROM UNTIL THE WHISTLE BLOWS: A COLLECTION OF GAMES, DANCES, AND ACTIVITIES FOR EIGHT- TO TWELVE-YEAR-OLDS © 1977 GOODYEAR PUBLISHING COMPANY, INC.

6

Forward Roll

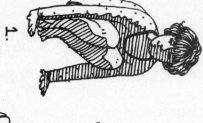

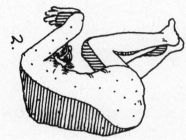

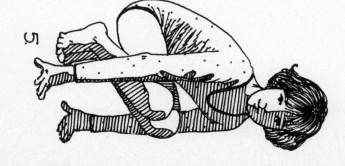

6

FROM UNTIL THE WHISTLE BLOWS: A COLLECTION OF GAMES, DANCES, AND ACTIVITIES FOR EIGHT- TO TWELVE-YEAR-OLDS © 1977 GOODYEAR PUBLISHING COMPANY, INC.

EVALUATION

Area: Stunts and Tumbling
Skills: Balance
Flexibility
Ability to Roll

Name _____ **Date** _____

Task	Check one or more
1. Crane Dive With your weight on one foot, your other foot extended to the rear, your arms along your sides, and your eyes looking forward, bend forward *slowly* and maintain for a count of 5. *Slowly* pick up a small object from the floor. Repeat.	Can establish position smoothly ☐ Shows control in change of position to pick up object ☐
2. Up and Over Lying on your back with your arms at your sides and your palms to the floor, lift your legs together slowly, keeping your knees straight. Touch your toes to the floor above your head. Return your legs slowly to their original position.	Keeps legs straight while lifting them ☐ Bends legs ☐ Can touch floor ☐ Cannot touch floor ☐ Maintains control while lowering legs to original position ☐
3. Forward Roll Assume a squat position. Tuck your head between your knees. Supporting your weight on your arms, roll forward, coming up to a standing position.	Takes correct starting position ☐ Nape of neck touches mat before head ☐ Rolls smoothly ☐ Rolls to feet without shoving off mat ☐ Supports weight on arms to begin roll ☐

Additional comments:

6

WARM-UP ACTIVITIES (for pages 156-170)

1. LIMBO

One-at-a-time, move under a stick or rope held off the ground. After everyone has had a turn at one height, lower the stick or rope. You'll have to change from an upright walk to a crouch, a knee walk, a crab walk, a crawl, and finally, to a crocodile crawl to get under without touching.

2. ALTERNATE TOE TOUCH

With your feet spread shoulder width and your arms extended straight out to the sides at shoulder height, bend at the waist to touch your right hand to your left foot, stand, then touch your left hand to your right foot. Repeat to a count of four: 1 (touch), 2 (stand), 3 (touch opposite), 4 (stand).

3. FOLLOW THE LEADER

Relying on verbal or sight cues alone, follow a leader who moves at changing speeds in a twisting, turning fashion while varying her posture by walking with her hands on her knees, holding her calves, holding her toes, crouching, standing on tiptoes and reaching, etc.

FROM UNTIL THE WHISTLE BLOWS: A COLLECTION OF GAMES, DANCES, AND ACTIVITIES FOR EIGHT- TO TWELVE-YEAR-OLDS © 1977 GOODYEAR PUBLISHING COMPANY, INC.

6

4.   LEG LIFT

- Lying on your back with your hands clasped behind your neck and keeping both legs stiff and straight, alternately lift one leg high off the floor, then the other.
- Try lifting both legs together slowly and then letting them down slowly.

5.   RUN IN PLACE

Standing in one place, alternately lift and lower your legs. Vary the height of your lift and the speed at which you move.

6.   CRISS CROSS WALK

- Standing, cross your left foot over your right foot, placing your ankles close together.
- Now cross your right foot over your left foot, ending with your ankles touching.
- Repeat this motion, moving forward in small steps and varying your speed.
- Have a Criss Cross Walk race.

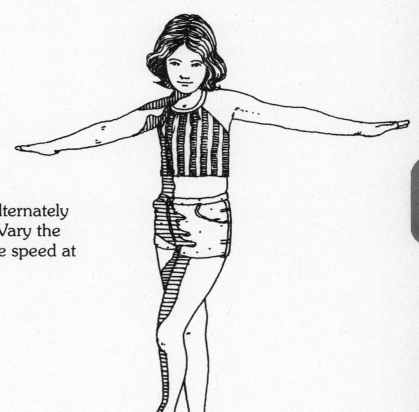

6

CRANE STAND   5 MIN.

Purpose: Developing agility, strength, balance
Equipment: None
Play Area: Clean, flat, smooth surface in a classroom, gym, or yard
Formation: Well-spaced free formation.

Directions:

While standing and extending your arms to the sides,
- wrap your left foot behind your right knee, bending your right leg *slightly* for balance. Hold for a count of 10.
- wrap your right foot behind your left knee, bending your left leg *slightly* for balance. Hold for a count of 10.

Practice to extend the length of time you can "hold."

Related Activities:

- Talk about cranes: What is a crane? Where do cranes live? What do they eat? What size (how tall) are they? How long are their legs? Can you *crane* your neck?
- What are stilts? If some are available, try them out.

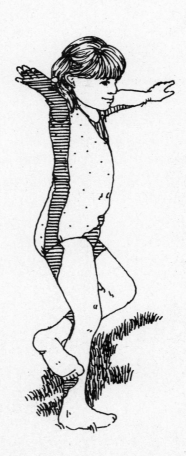

FROM *UNTIL THE WHISTLE BLOWS: A COLLECTION OF GAMES, DANCES, AND ACTIVITIES FOR EIGHT- TO TWELVE-YEAR-OLDS* © 1977 GOODYEAR PUBLISHING COMPANY, INC.

6

CRAB WALK   10 MIN.

Purpose: Developing agility, strength, balance
Equipment: None
Play Area: Clean, flat, smooth surface in a classroom, gym, or yard
Formation: Well-spaced lines or free formation; all moving in the same direction.

Directions:

- From a sitting position, lean back on your hands, lift your buttocks off the floor or ground, and "walk" in the direction of your feet or head, keeping your head and body in a straight line.
- To do the **lobster walk**, assume the same position but walk sideways (left or right).

Related Activities:

- Talk about shellfish: What is a *mollusk*? What is a *crustacean*? If one came to your house for dinner, would you feed him or eat him? What would you feed him? How would you eat him—raw, cooked, with fingers or fork?
- Encourage children to bring some seashells (labeled, if possible) to share in a collection.
- Talk about the ways animals move. Think of some words to describe animal locomotion (e.g., bound, scamper, slither, scuttle, wriggle).

6

HEEL SLAP   5 MIN.

Purpose: Developing agility, strength, balance
Equipment: None
Play Area: Clean, flat, smooth surface in a classroom, gym, or yard
Formation: Standing well spaced in a circle, lines, or free formation.

Directions:
- Bend your knees to help your spring.
- Holding your hands down at your sides, jump up and bend your knees so that you can slap your heels while in the air.

Vary the activity by
- increasing the number of slaps.
- making a quarter turn each time.
- doing it to a rhythmic count: jump once (1), jump and slap (2).

6

FROM *UNTIL THE WHISTLE BLOWS: A COLLECTION OF GAMES, DANCES, AND ACTIVITIES FOR EIGHT- TO TWELVE-YEAR-OLDS* © 1977 GOODYEAR PUBLISHING COMPANY, INC.

CORKSCREW

5 MIN.

Purpose: Developing strength, balance, agility
Equipment: None
Play Area: Clean, flat, smooth surface in a classroom, gym, or yard
Formation: Well-spaced free formation.

Directions:

- Spread your feet slightly.
- Tuck your left arm behind your back.
- Bending your knees and rising on your toes for balance, place your right arm across your body, behind your left knee, between your ankles, and touch the toes on your right foot.
- Tuck your right arm behind you, and try it with the left.

6

COFFEE GRINDER   5 MIN.

Purpose: Developing strength and balance
Equipment: None
Play Area: Clean, flat, smooth surface in a classroom, gym, or yard
Formation: Well-spaced lines.

Directions:

- Sit with your legs out straight in front of you and your hands, palms down, on the floor behind your hips.
- Roll to one side and raise your hips off the floor, supporting your weight on the hand and foot nearest the floor or ground.
- Taking small "steps" with your feet, pivot on the supporting arm, keeping it straight.
- Repeat the activity on the opposite side.
- Vary the speed of your turn.

Related Activities:

- Talk about coffee: From what is it made? Where are the beans grown? How are they processed?
- What other foods are processed by grinding?

FROM UNTIL THE WHISTLE BLOWS: A COLLECTION OF GAMES, DANCES, AND ACTIVITIES FOR EIGHT- TO TWELVE-YEAR-OLDS © 1977 GOODYEAR PUBLISHING COMPANY, INC.

6

SPINNER

5 MIN.

Purpose: Developing strength and balance
Equipment: None
Play Area: Clean, flat, *smooth* surface in a classroom or gym
Formation: Well-spaced lines, circle, or free formation.

Directions:
- Sit on the floor with your feet on the floor in front of you, your knees bent, and your hands, palms down, on the floor at your sides.
- Lifting your feet off the floor, placing your weight on your buttocks, and rocking back slightly, push with your hands to make your body spin.
- Now spin the other way.

Related Activities:
- Name some things that spin (e.g., a top, a spider).
- Name some things that are made by spinning (e.g., yarn, a web).
- Who wanted straw spun into gold?

6

FORWARD ROLL (review of page 151)　　10 MIN.

Purpose: Developing lead-up skills and flexibility
Equipment: Mats or thick blankets (folded)
Play Area: Gym, classroom (cleared), or yard
Formation: Children in line facing mats (2 or 3) placed end-to-end. You should watch and spot each child on his first few rolls.

Directions:
- Spread your feet slightly, squat down, and place your hands flat on the mat.
- Tuck your head between your legs.
- Pushing slightly with your feet, transfer your weight to your hands and roll forward in a tuck position.
- As your weight is transferred to the nape of your neck and then to your back, bring your arms forward to grasp your shins.
- Continue your roll until your feet are under you, then rise to a standing position.

- Vary by crossing your legs before your roll and keeping them crossed throughout.

Note:
The nape of the neck, not the head, should touch the mat first. If a child is rolling over one shoulder, have her spread her feet farther apart before beginning her roll.

To Spot:
"Lift" and push in the direction of the roll at the nape of the neck and on the shin.

6

FROM UNTIL THE WHISTLE BLOWS: A COLLECTION OF GAMES, DANCES, AND ACTIVITIES FOR EIGHT- TO TWELVE-YEAR-OLDS © 1977 GOODYEAR PUBLISHING COMPANY, INC.

FALLING   10 MIN.

Purpose: Developing lead-up skills, flexibility, spatial awareness
Equipment: Mats or thick blankets (folded)
Play Area: Gym, cleared classroom, or yard
Formation: Mats in well-spaced lines or a semicircle with children alongside.

Directions:
- Stand to the side of the mat.
- Fold your arms across your chest.
- Bend your knees slightly.
- Roll onto the mat, landing on the outside of your knee, on the side of your hip, and on your shoulder.

Note:
Be sure to have children keep their arms folded and out of the way.

Related Activities:
- Talk about the importance of rolling with a fall, keeping your hands and arms out of the way, and landing on your side.
- If possible observe, in movies, on television, or by visiting a movie studio, how professional stunt men take their falls. Thanks to television's "instant replay," children may be able to see this same technique used by professional football players and other athletes.

6

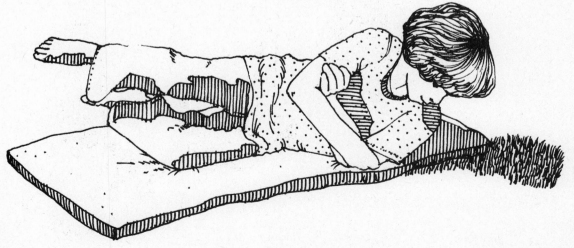

EGG ROLL   5 MIN.

Purpose: Developing lead-up skills, flexibility, spatial awareness
Equipment: Mats or thick blankets (folded)
Play Area: Gym, cleared classroom, or yard
Formation: Well-spaced lines next to one mat, or several mats placed in lines or a semicircle.

Directions:

- Squat down with your heels at the edge of the mat.
- Roll backward, placing your hands next to your head, palms down, with the fingers pointing to your shoulders.
- Rock back to your feet.
- Roll backward again, placing your hands next to your head, palms down.

- Touch your toes to the mat beyond your head and push with your hands so that you continue your motion, rolling over your head to end, as you began, in a squat position.

FROM UNTIL THE WHISTLE BLOWS: A COLLECTION OF GAMES, DANCES, AND ACTIVITIES FOR EIGHT- TO TWELVE-YEAR-OLDS © 1977 GOODYEAR PUBLISHING COMPANY, INC.

FROM *UNTIL THE WHISTLE BLOWS: A COLLECTION OF GAMES, DANCES, AND ACTIVITIES FOR EIGHT- TO TWELVE-YEAR-OLDS* © 1977 GOODYEAR PUBLISHING COMPANY, INC.

TWISTER   10 MIN.

Purpose: Developing balance, flexibility, strength, ability to work with a partner

Equipment: None

Play Area: Clean, flat, smooth surface in a classroom, gym, or yard

Formation: Pairs of partners in well-spaced free formation, designated "partner 1" and "partner 2."

Directions:
- Join right hands.
- Partner 1 swings his right leg over joined hands.
- Partner 2 swings his left leg over.
- Partner 1 swings his left leg over.
- Partner 2 swings his right leg over to end in beginning position, standing with right hands joined.
- Repeat, joining left hands and swinging the opposite leg over first.

6

FROG JUMP (variation) 10 MIN.

Purpose: Developing strength and coordination
Equipment: Mats or thick blankets (folded)
Play Area: Clean, flat, smooth surface in a classroom, gym, or yard
Formation: Well-spaced lines; all moving in one direction.

Directions:

- Assume a crouched position, placing your hands on the floor in front of your feet and supporting your weight equally on your hands and feet.
- Pushing off with your hands and feet, spring up and forward.
- Land with your weight evenly distributed on your arms and legs, allowing your elbows and knees to give slightly.
- Vary the height and distance of your jump.

6

FROM UNTIL THE WHISTLE BLOWS: A COLLECTION OF GAMES, DANCES, AND ACTIVITIES FOR EIGHT- TO TWELVE-YEAR-OLDS © 1977 GOODYEAR PUBLISHING COMPANY, INC.

TRIPOD   10 MIN.

Purpose: Developing strength, coordination
Equipment: Mats or thick blankets (folded)
Play Area: Clean, flat, smooth surface in a classroom, gym, or yard
Formation: Well-spaced on individual mats arranged in lines or in a semicircle.

Directions:
- Squat down on the mat.
- Place your hands on the mat about a shoulder width apart with your elbows inside your thighs.
- Keeping your elbows straight and pushing against your inner lower thighs, shift your weight slowly forward onto your arms.
- After you touch your forehead to the mat, return to your original position.

Note:
If children are having difficulty, suggest that they turn their fingers slightly away from their body.

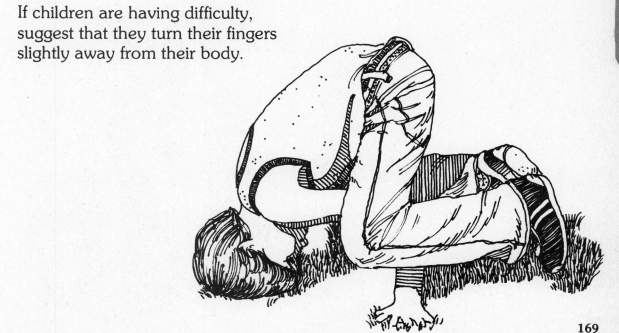

6

LEAP FROG   5 MIN.

Purpose: Developing strength, coordination
Equipment: Mats or thick blankets (folded)
Play Area: Clean, flat, smooth surface in a classroom (cleared), gym, or yard
Formation: Well-spaced lines with children 2 to 3 feet apart.

Directions:

- The first child in each line squats on all fours on the mat.
- The second child in line places his hands, palms down, on the back of the squatting child in front of him.
- Transferring his weight to his hands in a frog jump movement, he springs forward, straddling the crouched child and landing in front of him on the mat.
- Immediately, he also crouches.
- The third child in line now jumps over first child, then over the second child, and assumes a crouched position.
- Jumping is continued in this fashion until the last child in line has jumped over all those in front of him, or—if the lines are short—until each child in line has jumped over all the others.

FROM UNTIL THE WHISTLE BLOWS: A COLLECTION OF GAMES, DANCES, AND ACTIVITIES FOR EIGHT- TO TWELVE-YEAR-OLDS © 1977 GOODYEAR PUBLISHING COMPANY, INC.

EVALUATION

Area: Stunts and Tumbling
Skills: Strength
       Balance
       Safety

Name _____ **Date** _____

Task	Check one or more
1. Crab walk From a sitting position with your hands behind your buttocks, lift your buttocks off the floor. Walk forward and backward, keeping your body straight from the knees to the neck.	Has sufficient strength to support body ☐ Is unable to support body and move easily ☐ Moves forward and backward easily ☐
2. Coffee Grinder From a sitting position with your legs extended and your hands on the floor behind your hips, roll to one side and raise your hips off the floor, supporting your weight on one hand and foot. Keeping your body straight and pivoting on your hand, move in a circle, taking small "steps." Repeat on the opposite side.	Right arm and leg are strong enough to complete task ☐ Left arm and leg are strong enough to complete task ☐
3. The Fall With the side of one foot next to a mat, bend down slightly and roll onto the mat, keeping your arms crossed and landing on the side of your knee, hip, and shoulder. Repeat on your other side.	Movement is smooth and controlled ☐ Movement is not smooth and controlled ☐ Arms are kept out of the way—folded, protected ☐ Arms are under the fall ☐

Additional comments:

6

WARM-UP ACTIVITIES (for pages 175-186)

1. STEAM ENGINE
- Clasp your hands behind your neck.
- Step forward on your left leg, bringing your right knee up and bending your torso so that you can touch your right knee with your left elbow.
- Straightening up, step forward on your right foot.
- Repeat, stepping on your right foot, touching your left knee to your right elbow, straightening up while stepping forward on your left foot.

2. RUNNING THREES
- Three children hook elbows with the middle child facing in the opposite direction from the outside two.
- On cue, threesomes run forward or backward.

FROM *UNTIL THE WHISTLE BLOWS: A COLLECTION OF GAMES, DANCES, AND ACTIVITIES FOR EIGHT- TO TWELVE-YEAR-OLDS* © 1977 GOODYEAR PUBLISHING COMPANY, INC.

6

FROM UNTIL THE WHISTLE BLOWS: A COLLECTION OF GAMES, DANCES, AND ACTIVITIES FOR EIGHT- TO TWELVE-YEAR-OLDS ©1977 GOODYEAR PUBLISHING COMPANY, INC.

3. JUMPING MAZE

- Arrange colored squares on the floor or use chalk or masking tape to draw a hopscotch pattern.
- Tell children to jump from square to square in a particular sequence (e.g., "from red, to orange to yellow," or "from 1 to 2 to 3").
- Have children jump as high as possible; have them jump and touch an object.
- Stress good landings—on balls of feet (not flat-footed) with knees bent slightly to absorb shock.

4. HOPPER

Have children hop over an obstacle forward, backward, and sideways. Vary the height of the obstacle.

5. CIRCLES

Standing in place, make large or small circles (as directed) with your hands, arms, head, torso, left foot, left leg, right foot, right leg, or a combination of these.

6

WARM-UP ACTIVITIES (continued)

6. TWISTER
- Standing in place with your feet slightly apart and your arms extended straight out at shoulder level, twist your torso to the right, then to the left.
- Sitting on the floor or ground with your legs slightly apart and straight out in front of you and your arms extended straight out at shoulder level, twist your torso to the right, then to the left.
- Repeat in sitting position with legs crossed.

7. TOUCHING TOES
- Standing with your feet slightly apart and keeping your knees straight, bend from the waist to touch the floor or ground with your fingers.
- Walk your fingers forward and backward on the ground between your legs as far as you can without losing your balance or bending your knees.

FROM UNTIL THE WHISTLE BLOWS: A COLLECTION OF GAMES, DANCES, AND ACTIVITIES FOR EIGHT- TO TWELVE-YEAR-OLDS © 1977 GOODYEAR PUBLISHING COMPANY, INC.

6

BALANCED SIT   10 MIN.

Purpose: Developing strength, balance, flexibility
Equipment: None
Play Area: Clean, flat, smooth surface in a classroom (cleared), gym, or yard
Formation: Well-spaced lines, semicircle, or free formation.

Directions:

- While standing, hold your arms straight out in front of you at shoulder height.
- Lift your left leg and extend it straight out in front.
- In this balanced position, slowly lower your body by bending your right knee, but keeping your back straight, until you sit on your right heel.

- Return to a standing position.
- Repeat, lifting your right leg.
- As a variation, try sitting on the floor or ground rather than on your heel.

SEAL CRAWL   10 MIN.

Purpose: Developing strength, balance, flexibility
Equipment: Mats or thick blankets (folded)
Play Area: Clean, flat, smooth surface in a classroom (cleared), gym, or yard
Formation: Well-spaced lines or free formation; all moving in one direction.

Directions:

- Lie face down on mats or blankets with your legs straight, your elbows bent, and your hands placed, palms down, next to your shoulders.
- Push up with your arms so that your body is supported only by your toes and forearms.
- Keeping your legs straight and dragging your toes, "walk" forward by moving one arm, then the other.

Vary this activity by

- pushing up farther with your arms, so that your body is supported only by your hands and toes, and moving in the same manner.
- spreading your legs and alternately moving your hands and feet in a "turtle walk."
- turning over on your back, supporting your weight on your hands and heels, and dragging your heels.

Related Activities:

- Talk about *mammals*: What is a mammal? What is the largest living mammal? The smallest?
- Talk about mammals that can live both on land and in the sea: Name some. What do they eat? What do they breathe? How? Who are their natural enemies? When are they most vulnerable?
- Talk about swimming and water safety.

6

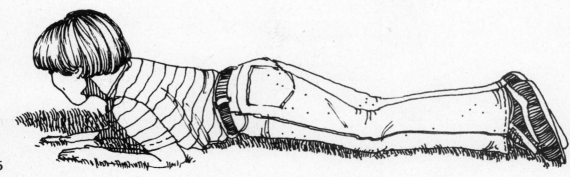

FROM UNTIL THE WHISTLE BLOWS: A COLLECTION OF GAMES, DANCES, AND ACTIVITIES FOR EIGHT- TO TWELVE-YEAR-OLDS © 1977 GOODYEAR PUBLISHING COMPANY, INC.

HAND-KNEE BALANCE

10 MIN.

Purpose: Developing balance, general endurance, strength
Equipment: 1 mat or thick blanket (folded) per child
Play Area: Clean, flat, smooth surface in a classroom (cleared), gym, or yard
Formation: Well-spaced lines, semicircle, or free formation; all kneeling on mats.

Directions:

- Kneel on your mat and put your hands, palms down, on the mat directly beneath your shoulders.
- With your toes pointed behind you and your weight supported by your hands and knees, lift your left leg and your right hand and hold.

- Now raise your right hand also and balance on your right knee-shin-foot alone.
- Repeat, lifting your right leg and left hand, then your right hand so that you balance on your left knee-shin-foot.

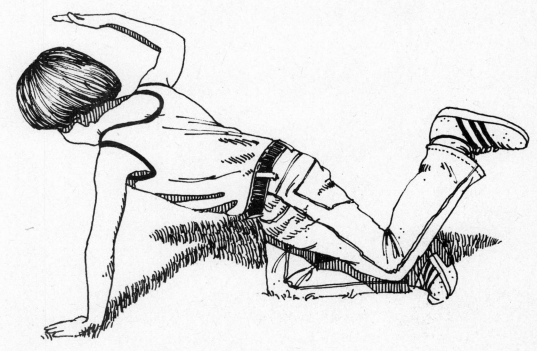

6

JUMP FROM KNEES   10 MIN.

Purpose: Developing balance, general endurance, strength
Equipment: 1 mat or thick blanket (folded) per child
Play Area: Clean, flat, smooth surface in a classroom (cleared), gym, or yard
Formation: On mats in well-spaced lines or semicircle.

Directions:
- Kneel on your mat with your weight on your knees-shins-feet, your back straight, and your body erect.
- Swing your arms forward and up, using the momentum of your arm swing to lift your body to your feet and then on up to a standing position.

Related Activities:
- Talk about *momentum*.
- Have children turn in place with their arms extended straight out at the shoulders, then with them extended straight down at their sides or folded across their torso.
- If possible, watch an ice skater do a spin. Notice especially how he uses his arms to increase and decrease his spin speed.

6

FROM UNTIL THE WHISTLE BLOWS: A COLLECTION OF GAMES, DANCES, AND ACTIVITIES FOR EIGHT- TO TWELVE-YEAR-OLDS © 1977 GOODYEAR PUBLISHING COMPANY, INC.

BLIND TOUCH

5 MIN.

Purpose: Developing balance, general endurance, strength
Equipment: (Optional) 1 mat or thick blanket (folded) per child
Play Area: Clean, flat, smooth surface in a classroom (cleared), gym, or yard.
Formation: On mats or floor in well-spaced lines or semicircle.

Directions:
- While standing, reach in back of you to grasp your left wrist with your right hand, keeping your left elbow straight.
- Point one finger of your left hand to the floor.
- Keeping your back straight, bending your knees, and looking straight ahead (not down), slowly descend to the floor, touch your finger to it, and return to a standing position.
- Repeat, grasping your right wrist with your left hand.

6

TUMMY BALANCE

5 MIN.

Purpose: Developing balance, strength, flexibility
Equipment: (Optional) 1 mat or thick blanket (folded) per child
Play Area: Clean, flat, smooth surface in a classroom (cleared), gym, or yard
Formation: On mats or floor in well-spaced lines or semicircle.

Directions:

- Lying prone on your mat or on the floor, stretch your arms forward with your palms down.
- Keeping your knees and elbows straight, lift your legs, head, chest, and arms off the floor and balance on your stomach.

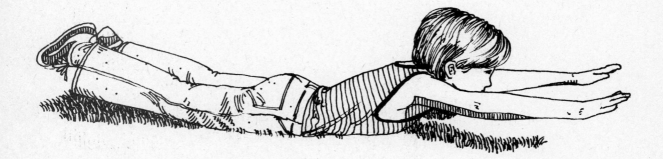

FROM UNTIL THE WHISTLE BLOWS: A COLLECTION OF GAMES, DANCES, AND ACTIVITIES FOR EIGHT- TO TWELVE-YEAR-OLDS © 1977 GOODYEAR PUBLISHING COMPANY, INC.

EGG ROLL (review of page 164) 5 MIN.

Purpose: Developing balance, strength, flexibility
Equipment: 1 mat or thick blanket (folded) per child
Play Area: Clean, flat, smooth surface in a classroom (cleared), gym, or yard
Formation: On mats in well-spaced lines or semicircle.

Directions:
- Squat with your heels against the end of the mat.
- Roll backward, placing your hands, palms down, beside your head with your fingers pointing toward your shoulders.
- Roll backward again, placing your hands next to your head, palms down.
- This time, touch your toes to the floor beyond your head.
- Continue pushing with your hands so that you roll over to a squat position.

Related Activities:
- Roll an egg and let the children watch.
- What shape is an egg?
- Spin a hardboiled egg and a raw egg. Which one can be spun more successfully? Why?

6

BACKWARD ROLL

5 MIN.

Purpose: Developing balance, strength, flexibility
Equipment: Mats or thick blankets (folded)
Play Area: Clean, flat, smooth surface in a classroom (cleared), gym, or yard
Formation: In a line facing mats placed end-to-end. Have each child turn his back to the mat and stand with his heels against the edge to ensure room for movement.

Directions:

- Squat with your heels against the edge of the mat, placing your hands (palms down, thumbs in) on the floor at shoulder width.
- Remaining in a tuck position, push off with the balls of your feet and roll backward, bending your elbows and bringing your hands, palms up, alongside your head. Your thumbs should be pointing toward your ears.
- When your shoulders and head touch the mat, push with your hands and straighten your elbows, taking your body weight off your neck onto your arms.
- Roll on over to end in a squat position.
- Do a series of rolls down the mats.

To Spot:

- As a child rolls and his hips come up in the air, grasp them and lift to guide the roll and lighten the load on his neck.
- Watch that each child maintains a tuck position and lifts with his arms.

Related Activities:

Talk about the body, especially those parts that are weak or vulnerable to pressure or blows, and ways to protect it (e.g., letting your extended arms—with elbows held straight and stiff—precede your body into the water in a dive to protect your head and neck).

6

182

FROM UNTIL THE WHISTLE BLOWS: A COLLECTION OF GAMES, DANCES, AND ACTIVITIES FOR EIGHT- TO TWELVE-YEAR-OLDS © 1977 GOODYEAR PUBLISHING COMPANY, INC.

MULE KICK
10 MIN.

Purpose: Developing strength, endurance, balance
Equipment: 1 mat or thick blanket (folded) per child
Play Area: Clean, flat, smooth surface in a classroom (cleared), gym, or yard
Formation: Well-spaced lines or semicircle.

Directions:
- Stand facing your mat with your toes at the edge.
- Bending from the waist, place your hands, palms down, on the mat, kicking your legs (ankles together) up and taking your weight momentarily onto your arms.
- Return to your original position.

Note:
Caution children *not* to jump so high that they lose their balance, but show them how to tuck and roll (rather than pivoting from the wrists) if they do overjump.

6

WHEELBARROW   15 MIN.

Purpose: Developing strength, endurance, and balance
Equipment: 1 mat or thick blanket (folded) per child
Play Area: Clean, flat, smooth surface in a classroom (cleared), gym, or yard
Formation: In twos, well spaced; all moving in the same direction.

Directions:
- One child bends from the waist, supporting his weight on his hands and feet (spread slightly apart).
- His partner steps between the first child's feet, grasps his knees, and lifts his legs off the floor to waist height.
- With the child in front setting the speed, partners "walk" forward.

Note:
This stunt is most successfully done when partners are of nearly the same height and weight and is not recommended for overweight children.

Related Activities:
- Talk about lifting and carrying heavy objects and the importance of bending your knees, keeping your back straight, and letting your legs (thighs) do the work.
- Talk about posture as a way of carrying the body's weight correctly—or incorrectly. Use the section in Chapter 8 for ideas.

6

FROM UNTIL THE WHISTLE BLOWS: A COLLECTION OF GAMES, DANCES, AND ACTIVITIES FOR EIGHT- TO TWELVE-YEAR-OLDS © 1977 GOODYEAR PUBLISHING COMPANY, INC.

ROCKING HORSE 10 MIN.

Purpose: Developing balance and the ability to work with a partner
Equipment: Mats or thick blankets (folded)
Play Area: Clean, flat, smooth surface in a classroom (cleared), gym, or yard
Formation: In twos on mats in well-spaced lines or semicircle with *shoes off*.

Directions:
- Partners face each other on their mat, each sitting on the other's toes (*not* feet or ankles), and grasp each other's forearms. (One partner's knees will be between the other's knees.)
- To begin rocking, one partner leans back, raising the other off the floor.
- Keeping their legs straight, they rock back in the other direction, and then forth and back.

Note:
This stunt is most easily done rhythmically so that the movement is continuous.

6

CHINESE GET UP   10 MIN.

Purpose: Developing balance and the ability to work with a partner
Equipment: Mats or thick blankets (folded)
Play Area: Clean, flat, smooth surface in a classroom (cleared), gym, or yard
Formation: In twos on mats in well-spaced lines or semicircle.

Directions:

- Partners stand back-to-back on their mat, hooking their elbows.
- Each placing her feet slightly in front of her and leaning gently against the other, they sit down slowly, bending their knees.
- When seated, they draw their feet up, placing their heels against their buttocks, and push against each other to rise.

Vary this stunt by
- using threesomes or foursomes instead of twosomes.
- going half way down and stopping to "hold that pose."
- moving like a spider.
- pulling up. Partners sit on mats facing each other with their feet flat on the mats and their toes touching. Grasping each other's forearms, they pull against each other to rise.

Note:

This stunt is most successfully done when partners are of nearly the same height and weight.

Related Activities:

- Talk about *insects*: What is an insect? Is a spider an insect? How do you know? Is an earthworm an insect? What about a caterpillar? How do insects move? Where do they live? What do they eat? Are they "good" or "bad"? Do some insects help us? (E.g., bee, ladybug, praying mantis.) How?
- If possible, observe some insects working (ants or bees), eating (caterpillars), and moving.

6

FROM UNTIL THE WHISTLE BLOWS: A COLLECTION OF GAMES, DANCES, AND ACTIVITIES FOR EIGHT- TO TWELVE-YEAR-OLDS © 1977 GOODYEAR PUBLISHING COMPANY, INC.

EVALUATION

Area: Stunts and Tumbling
Skills: Strength
Balance
Flexibility

Name _____ Date _____

Task	Check one or more
1. Seal Crawl From a prone position with your face down and your palms just above your shoulders, push up, keeping your legs straight, and "walk," dragging your toes and supporting your weight on your hands and toes.	Has sufficient strength to complete task ☐ Cannot maintain position and movement ☐
2. Knee Balance On all fours on a mat with your toes pointed backward, lift one leg and the opposite hand and maintain this balanced position. Lift your other hand and balance on one knee-shin-foot only.	Movements are smooth and controlled ☐ Cannot maintain balance ☐
3. Backward Roll From a squat position, push off with the balls of your feet and roll backward, placing your hands (palms down, thumbs pointing to your ears) alongside your head and straightening your elbows to take your weight off your neck. Roll on over to end in a squat position.	Starts from correct position ☐ Starts from incorrect position ☐ Maintains tuck ☐ Does not maintain tuck ☐ Hand position is correct ☐ Straightens arms to take weight off neck ☐

Additional comments:

6

GAMES

7.

Games are an important part of any activity education program. They help children learn to cooperate in a group or team effort, taking turns, following directions, and enjoying the company of others. They add fun and entertainment to the program. Ideally, they should also offer all children an opportunity to participate.

This chapter includes games involving locomotor and nonlocomotor skills; games to reinforce number concepts, color and shape recognition, and throwing and catching skills; and games appropriate for indoor, outdoor, classroom, gym, or yard use.

The basic equipment needed for these games includes:
- colored paper cut into geometric shapes
- balls
- 1 beanbag per child
- 8-foot rope
- a chair
- a chalkboard eraser
- 4 wastebaskets
- a blindfold

Before teaching a new game, complete all preparations (drawing or establishing boundaries, rounding up equipment), and give children an opportunity to practice the locomotor or nonlocomotor skill involved. To keep the children interested and alert throughout the game, give directions with enthusiasm and enforce rules with impartiality. After the children understand and have played the game several times, introduce a variation.

The lessons in this chapter are arranged from simple, beginning play activities to more complex games, sometimes involving skills used in more difficult games and sports. You may find it necessary to modify the tasks in each game to suit the ages and capabilities of the children playing. Demonstrations and/or chalkboard diagrams of the game may be useful in clarifying the directions.

7

COLORS   10-20 MIN.

Purpose: Developing locomotor skills, learning to follow directions
Equipment: 5 colors of paper cut into geometric shapes
Play Area: Gym, classroom, or yard
Formation: Seated in a single, large circle.

Directions:
- Pass out the colored shapes.
- Name one color and tell all who have that color to stand and run counterclockwise around the circle and back to their original places.
- Repeat each color several times.

Note:
Vary this activity by
- having children skip, gallop, hop, and leap.
- having children exchange colors.
- using shape as the identification point.

Related Activities:
Use numbers instead of colors.

FROM UNTIL THE WHISTLE BLOWS: A COLLECTION OF GAMES, DANCES, AND ACTIVITIES FOR EIGHT- TO TWELVE-YEAR-OLDS © 1977 GOODYEAR PUBLISHING COMPANY, INC.

7

KNEELING TAG   20 MIN.

Purpose: Developing locomotor skills
Equipment: None
Play Area: Yard or gym
Formation: Free formation; children spread out around the yard or gym.

Directions:
- Choose two to be "it."
- Those who are "it" attempt to tag the other children.
- Children can be "safe" by kneeling on one or both knees.
- At first, specify only "one knee" or "two knees." Later, specify "right knee" or "left knee," and make it clear that players kneeling on the wrong knee are *not* safe.

Related Activities:
Other activities to help with left–right identification and the development of listening skills.

TOSS THE BALL

15-20 MIN.

Purpose: Developing throwing and catching skills
Equipment: 1 ball per group
Play Area: Gym, yard
Formation: Groups of 6 to 8 in small circles with one child in the center of each circle.

Directions:

- Give the child in the center a ball.
- The center player throws the ball to each child in turn around the circle.
- Each child returns the ball to the center player.
- Give each child a chance to be in the center.

7

FROM *UNTIL THE WHISTLE BLOWS: A COLLECTION OF GAMES, DANCES, AND ACTIVITIES FOR EIGHT- TO TWELVE-YEAR-OLDS* © 1977 GOODYEAR PUBLISHING COMPANY, INC.

JUMP THE SHOT   20 MIN.

Purpose: Developing locomotor skills
Equipment: 8-foot rope, beanbag
Play Area: Gym, yard
Formation: Single circle facing the oncoming rope and beanbag; one
child stands in the center holding a rope with a beanbag
tied to one end.

Directions:

- Keeping the beanbag on the floor, the player in the center swings the rope in a large circle.
- As the beanbag comes close to those players standing in the circle, they jump to avoid being hit by it.
- Anyone who is hit must move away from the circle.
- The last remaining player becomes the one in the center for the next round.

Note:

Insist that the beanbag stay on the floor and the jumpers stay in a circle.

7

CUT THE CAKE   15-20 MIN.

Purpose: Locomotor activities
Equipment: None
Play Area: Classroom, gym, yard
Formation: Children in a single circle, hands joined, facing in.

Directions:

- One child is "it" and is called "the knife."
- With both hands he "cuts the cake" by tapping the hands of two adjacent children.
- These two children run in opposite directions around the circle.
- The knife stands still and judges which one returns to his starting position first.
- The winning runner is the new knife, and the old knife takes his place in the circle.

Related Activities:

- Talk about cakes: What are cakes made of? What makes a cake rise? On what occasions do we serve/eat cake? (E.g., birthdays, weddings.)
- Talk about birthdays and birth dates.
- Read *Happy Birthday to You!* by Dr. Seuss (New York: Random House, 1959).
- Bake a cake. Depending on how ambitious you want to be, this can be a simple add-water-to-a-mix activity or a lesson in following directions and metric measurement.
- Share your cake with others at a party.
- Have children design their "dream cakes" based on a theme such as a holiday (Halloween, Christmas, Valentine's Day, Easter), a zoo or circus, a favorite television show, their hobbies, or what they want to be when they grow up.
- Hold a cake-decorating contest *for children*.
- Visit a bakery.

7

FROM *UNTIL THE WHISTLE BLOWS: A COLLECTION OF GAMES, DANCES, AND ACTIVITIES FOR EIGHT- TO TWELVE-YEAR-OLDS* © 1977 GOODYEAR PUBLISHING COMPANY, INC.

7

DOGGIE AND BONE

20 MIN.

Purpose: Quiet activity
Equipment: Chair for "Doggie" to sit in; an eraser to be "the bone"
Play Area: Classroom
Formation: Children seated in a semicircle with "Doggie" in a chair on the empty side of the circle, his back to the other players; "bone" placed under Doggie's chair.

Directions:

- Doggie closes her eyes.
- Silently choose one of the children to sneak up, "steal" the bone from Doggie, return to his place, and sit on the bone.
- All the children chant,
    Doggie, Doggie, where's your bone?
    Somebody took it away from home.
- Doggie faces the circle and has three guesses to identify who took her bone. She asks, "(Name), did you take my bone?" The child replies, "No, Doggie (Yes, Doggie), I didn't take (I took) your bone."
- If Doggie guesses correctly, the one who took the bone becomes Doggie. Otherwise, Doggie hides her eyes again.

Note:

Keep the game moving. Change Doggies after two or three times if Doggie still does not guess correctly.

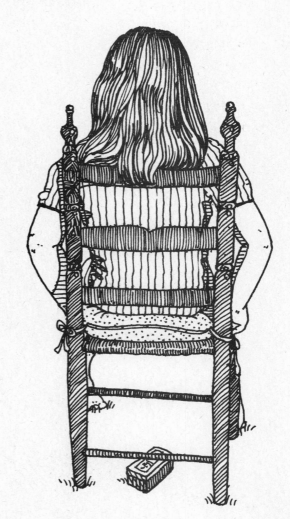

FROM UNTIL THE WHISTLE BLOWS: A COLLECTION OF GAMES, DANCES, AND ACTIVITIES FOR EIGHT- TO TWELVE-YEAR-OLDS © 1977 GOODYEAR PUBLISHING COMPANY, INC.

SQUIRREL IN THE TREE   20 MIN.

Purpose: Locomotor activities
Equipment: None
Play Area: Gym or yard
Formation: Players break up into groups of three and are numbered 1, 2, and 3 within each threesome. Facing each other, players 1 and 2 join hands to form a "tree." Player 3 is the "squirrel" and ducks under one pair of joined hands to get "in" the tree. Extra players are squirrels without trees.

Directions:

- When the leader calls, "Run, squirrel, run," all squirrels leave their trees to seek a new tree.
- Squirrels without trees try to get into a tree ahead of the other running players.
- After several turns, change positions of players so that everyone has a chance to be a squirrel.

Related Activities:

- Talk about squirrels: Where do they live? What do they eat? What sound do they make? How do they move?
- What is a *rodent*?

7

WHO IS MISSING?   20 MIN.

Purpose: Quiet activity
Equipment: None
Play Area: Classroom, gym
Formation: Children sit in their seats or in a circle.

Directions:
- Choose one child to be "it" and hide his eyes.
- Choose another child to leave the playing area.
- After this child has left, have the remaining children change seats with one another.
- Give the child who is "it" three chances to guess who is missing.
- If he guesses correctly, the child who was hiding becomes "it." If he does not guess correctly, he is "it" again.

7

FROM UNTIL THE WHISTLE BLOWS: A COLLECTION OF GAMES, DANCES, AND ACTIVITIES FOR EIGHT- TO TWELVE-YEAR-OLDS © 1977 GOODYEAR PUBLISHING COMPANY, INC.

CHARLIE OVER THE WATER   15-20 MIN.

Purpose: Locomotor activities
Equipment: None
Play Area: Classroom, gym, or yard
Formation: Children in a circle with one player, "Charlie," in the center.

Directions:
- Children in the circle walk around Charlie as they chant:
  Charlie over the water.
  Charlie over the sea.
  Charlie caught a big fish,
  But he can't catch me!
- As they say "me," all children in the circle sit down quickly.
- Charlie tries to catch one before he sits down.
- The child who is caught becomes Charlie.

Related Activities:
- Talk about fish: Where do fish live? What do they eat? What do they breathe? (I.e., oxygen their gills extract from the water.)
- Talk about water pollution: How do bodies of water become polluted? What effects do different kinds of pollution have on the fish in the water? On us?
- Read about the requirements of different kinds of fish, then set up an aquarium. If yours is to be a "community tank," that is, if it is to house fish of several species, select fish of compatible size and aggressiveness so that the small ones do not simply become a meal for the large ones. If you want only one species, guppies are small but brightly colored, very active, quite hardy, and relatively inexpensive. They are also live bearers and, once mature, reproduce readily at six-week intervals.

7

HIT THE BUCKET

20-25 MIN.

Purpose: Developing throwing skills
Equipment: 1 ball and a wastebasket or bucket for each group of 6 to 8 children
Play Area: Gym or yard
Formation: Groups of 6 to 8 in small circles with one child in the center of each circle.

Directions:
- In turn, each player tries to throw the ball into the bucket placed in center of each circle.
- The player in the center is the retriever: he gets the ball and passes it to the next player.
- After all players have had two (or more) turns, the retriever changes places with one of the children in the circle.

Note:
Give each child an opportunity to be the retriever. You might award a point for each "bucket" and let the child with the most points after a specified length of time become the new retriever.

FROM UNTIL THE WHISTLE BLOWS: A COLLECTION OF GAMES, DANCES, AND ACTIVITIES FOR EIGHT- TO TWELVE-YEAR-OLDS © 1977 GOODYEAR PUBLISHING COMPANY, INC.

7

RED ROVER   15-25 MIN.

Purpose: Developing locomotor skills
Equipment: None, but you will need to mark or designate two
boundary lines
Play Area: Gym or yard
Formation: Children stand on one line. "Red Rover" faces them
standing on another line.

Directions:
- Red Rover says, "Red Rover, Red Rover, let (name) come over."
- The child who is called must run across to the other line.
- Red Rover chases each child called, and each child caught stays in the center to help Red Rover catch the other players.
- The last one caught is the new Red Rover.

FROM UNTIL THE WHISTLE BLOWS: A COLLECTION OF GAMES, DANCES, AND ACTIVITIES FOR EIGHT- TO TWELVE-YEAR-OLDS © 1977 GOODYEAR PUBLISHING COMPANY, INC.

7

OLD MOTHER WITCH   15-20 MIN.

Purpose: Developing locomotor skills
Equipment: None, but designate a line or fence as "home base"
Play Area: Yard or gym

Directions:

- Choose one child to be Old Mother Witch and walk ahead.
- Other children follow along behind her in a well-spaced line, chanting:

  Old Mother Witch
  Fell in the ditch,
  Picked up a penny,
  And thought she was rich.

- The witch turns suddenly and pretends she is going to chase them, but goes on her way.

- When she has walked a long way from home base, she turns quickly and really chases them.
- Those the witch catches must help her catch the others. The last to be caught becomes the new Old Mother Witch.

Related Activities:

Discuss the terms "ditch" and "rich."

FROM UNTIL THE WHISTLE BLOWS: A COLLECTION OF GAMES, DANCES, AND ACTIVITIES FOR EIGHT- TO TWELVE-YEAR-OLDS © 1977 GOODYEAR PUBLISHING COMPANY, INC.

BLIND MAN'S BLUFF

20-25 MIN.

Purpose: Locomotor activities
Equipment: Blindfold
Play Area: Gym or yard in which an area 25 feet square has been marked off

Directions:

- Have children spread out over the playing area.
- Blindfold one player, turn him around three times, and then let him try to tag one of the other players.
- The players may move around, but they must stay inside the marked off area.
- The first one touched by the "Blind Man" takes his place.

TOUCH THE BALL

15-20 MIN.

Purpose: Developing throwing skills
Equipment: Ball
Play Area: Yard or gym
Formation: Children form a circle with "it" inside.

Directions:

- As the ball is passed around and across the circle, the child who is "it" must try to touch the ball.
- When he does, whoever threw the ball or touched it last becomes "it," and the original "it" takes his place in the circle.

Note:

Keep the ball moving. Throw it as often as possible and to a different person each time.

FROM UNTIL THE WHISTLE BLOWS: A COLLECTION OF GAMES, DANCES, AND ACTIVITIES FOR EIGHT- TO TWELVE-YEAR-OLDS © 1977 GOODYEAR PUBLISHING COMPANY, INC.

HAVE YOU SEEN MY SHEEP? 20 MIN.

Purpose: Locomotor activities
Equipment: None
Play Area: Yard or gym
Formation: Children seated in a circle; one player chosen to be "it."

Directions:

- As the player who is "it" walks around the outside of the circle, she stops behind one of the players and asks, "Have you seen my sheep?"
- The player she asks replies, "What does it look like?"
- The child who is "it" then describes another player in the circle.
- The child she asked tries to guess who is being described.

- When she guesses correctly, she chases the player who was described around the outside of the circle. If she tags that player before he returns to his place, the tagged player becomes "it." If she does not tag him, the game is repeated with the chaser being "it."
- The first "it" takes the place of the chaser.

7

KEEP IT UP

20-25 MIN.

Purpose: Developing ball handling skills
Equipment: 1 ball for each group
Play Area: Yard or gym
Formation: Groups or teams of 5 or 6 in small circles.

Directions:

- At the signal, a team member tosses the ball into play.
- The players try to keep the ball in the air by batting it with open hands. The ball must not be caught or hit; it must be batted as is a setup in volleyball.
- The team who keeps its ball up the longest wins a point.
- The team earning the most points during the time allotted for play wins the game.

Note:

Do not keep score until players are able to keep the ball in play for some time.

FROM *UNTIL THE WHISTLE BLOWS: A COLLECTION OF GAMES, DANCES, AND ACTIVITIES FOR EIGHT- TO TWELVE-YEAR-OLDS* ©1977 GOODYEAR PUBLISHING COMPANY, INC.

JAPANESE TAG

15-20 MIN.

Purpose: Locomotor activities
Equipment: None
Play Area: Yard or gym
Formation: Well-spaced free formation with one child chosen to be "it."

Directions:

- The player who is "it" moves about until he tags another child with his hand.
- The player tagged by "it" puts one hand on the spot where "it" touched him (his back, leg, etc.) and tries to tag someone else with his other hand.
- The last player tagged is "it" for the next game.

Note:

Limit the area of play to make it more difficult to avoid being tagged.

CENTER BASE

15-25 MIN.

Purpose: Developing tossing and catching skills
Equipment: Ball; playing circle with small circle marked in center of it
Play Area: Yard or gym
Formation: Children in large circle with "it" inside small circle.

Directions:

- "It" tosses the ball to a player in the circle.
- The player catches the ball and brings it to the center of the circle where she places it inside the small circle.
- Then she chases "it." Both runner and chaser must run to the outside of the circle through the space left by the player who put the ball inside the small circle.

- The runner is safe when he comes back into the circle through this same space and touches the ball.
- If the chaser tags the runner, the runner is "it" again. If she does not tag him, the chaser becomes "it."

Note:

Encourage the children to let all have a turn.

FROM UNTIL THE WHISTLE BLOWS: A COLLECTION OF GAMES, DANCES, AND ACTIVITIES FOR EIGHT- TO TWELVE-YEAR-OLDS © 1977 GOODYEAR PUBLISHING COMPANY, INC.

FROM UNTIL THE WHISTLE BLOWS: A COLLECTION OF GAMES, DANCES, AND ACTIVITIES FOR EIGHT- TO TWELVE-YEAR-OLDS ©1977 GOODYEAR PUBLISHING COMPANY, INC.

DODGE BALL

15-25 MIN.

Purpose: Developing locomotor, nonlocomotor, and ball handling skills
Equipment: Soft rubber ball
Play Area: Yard or gym
Formation: Two-thirds of the group form a large circle around the remaining players.

Directions:

- The players around the circle attempt to hit those inside the circle *below the waist* with the ball.
- When a player is hit, he exchanges places with the player who hit him.
- Repeat the game until all players have had an opportunity to dodge the ball.

- When the ball goes outside the circle, the closest player recovers it and brings it back to resume the game.

Note:
Emphasize to the children that they are to dodge or jump to avoid being hit as long as possible.

7

THE BUILDING BLOCKS OF PHYSICAL LIFE

8.

Most children grow up without learning about how their bodies grow, work, and play, and how they can best be maintained. Yet such knowledge should be a part of every child's education. And the earlier in life this learning occurs, the greater the opportunity for its use to direct or even correct development and to achieve health and happiness.

Why not learn to identify parts of the body as soon as possible?

These beginning "building blocks" have been arranged so that the pages may be removed and placed on a bulletin board or even reproduced for individual study. The first building block contains elementary information about the human body.

THE HUMAN CELL

The **cell** is the body's basic structural unit. Every part of the body is composed of millions of tiny cells. There are skin cells, muscle cells, blood cells, nerve cells, and bone cells. Each varies in size and shape, depending upon the tissue it composes and the function it performs. Every cell is capable of reproducing itself, and it is through this process of cell reproduction (usually **mitosis**) that the body grows and that damaged or worn out cells are replaced.

Each cell requires food and oxygen and must have its waste products removed so that it will not be poisoned by them. Exercise stimulates blood circulation and thus the feeding of the cells and the removal of their waste products. Inadequate food, water, oxygen, or rest may cause cells to become sick.

Similar cells are grouped together to form **tissues**. There are four basic kinds of tissue in everyone:

- **epithelial**—comprises the skin and covers the openings in the body
- **connective**—holds different parts of the body together
- **nervous**—forms the communications network on which messages are sent throughout the body
- **muscle**—on which all movement depends

Two or more tissues grouped together to perform certain functions are called **organs**. Some of your body's organs are the heart, lungs, brain, eyes, liver, kidneys, stomach, and intestine. Each organ has a very special job to do and can do its job best when it is healthy. The health of all tissues and organs depends upon nutrition, exercise, and freedom from disease.

8

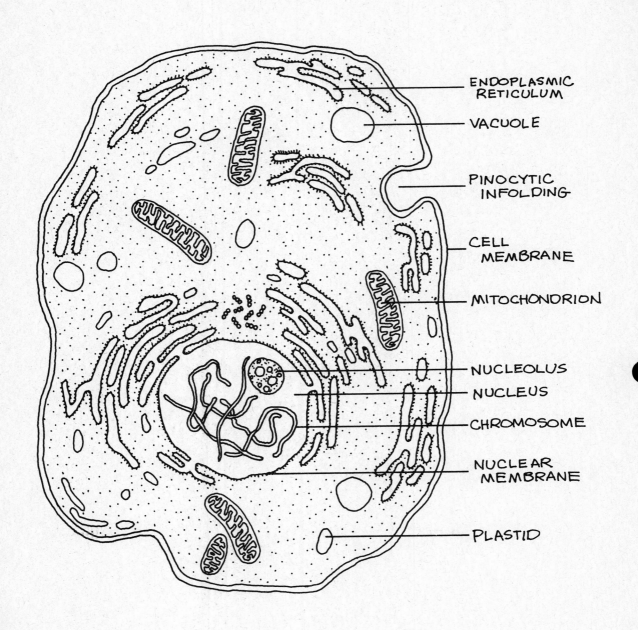

ENDOPLASMIC
RETICULUM

VACUOLE

PINOCYTIC
INFOLDING

CELL
MEMBRANE

MITOCHONDRION

NUCLEOLUS

NUCLEUS

CHROMOSOME

NUCLEAR
MEMBRANE

PLASTID

THE HUMAN CELL

SYSTEMS

A **system** is an arrangement of organs concerned with the same function. The major systems of the body are:

- **skeletal** (bones)
- **muscular** (muscles)
- **cardiovascular** (heart, arteries, veins, blood)
- **lymphatic** (lymph, lymph nodes and vessels)
- **endocrine** (a number of ductless glands)
- **respiratory** (lungs)
- **nervous** (brain and nerves)
- **digestive** (alimentary canal and its accessories)
- **reproductive** (organs used in making new life)

All of these systems work together to keep the body alive and functioning properly.

8

THE SKELETAL SYSTEM

The human body is composed of some 206 bones termed **axial** (skull, backbone, and ribs) or **appendicular** (arms, legs, hips, and shoulders). The total human bone framework or skeleton supports the soft tissues and protects the delicate organs, such as the heart, spinal cord, lungs, and brain.

Bones also serve as levers for movement. They are primarily a dense form of connective tissue. The inorganic material—chiefly calcium phosphate—they contain makes them hard, while the protein in them gives them their flexibility. Strong, healthy bones depend upon sufficient exercise and upon adequate calcium in the diet. Milk is a good source of calcium, as are almonds, cheese, and leafy vegetables.

Related Activities:

- If possible, obtain (perhaps from your butcher or from a can of salmon) some bones and examine them. Note particularly their texture and strength and the way vertebrae fit together to form the backbone or spine.
- What is a bone break called? (A fracture.) How are bones broken? How can you avoid this type of injury? How does a doctor determine that a bone is broken? What does he do to help it heal properly?
- If possible, obtain and look at X-rays of healthy, broken, and healed bones.
- Do insects have a skeleton?
- What is a **vertebrate?** An **invertebrate?**
- What would you study in **osteology?**
- What is **ossification?**
- If we say someone's mind has **ossified**, what do we mean? (I.e., that it has become hardened or resistant to new ideas.)
- Where is the smallest bone in the human body? (Inside the ear.)
- Where is the largest bone in the human body? (In the thigh.) What is it called? (The **femur**.)

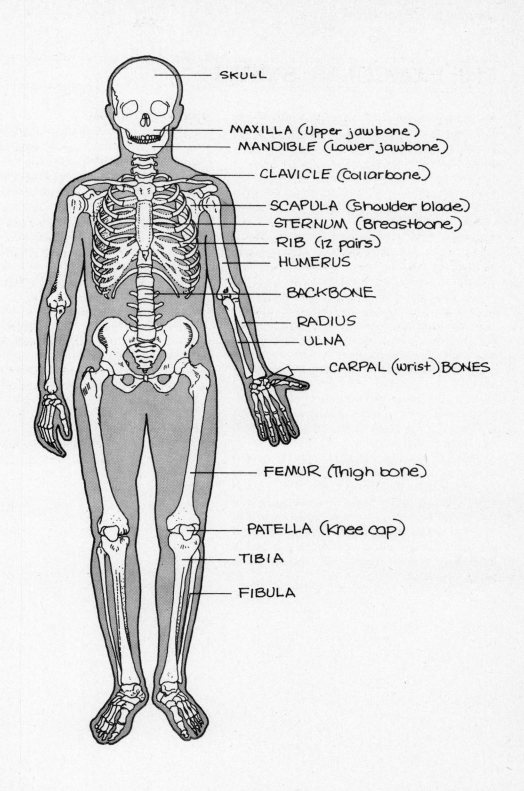

SKULL

MAXILLA (Upper jawbone)
MANDIBLE (Lower jawbone)
CLAVICLE (Collarbone)
SCAPULA (Shoulder blade)
STERNUM (Breastbone)
RIB (12 pairs)
HUMERUS
BACKBONE
RADIUS
ULNA
CARPAL (Wrist) BONES
FEMUR (Thigh bone)
PATELLA (Knee cap)
TIBIA
FIBULA

THE SKELETAL SYSTEM

FROM *UNTIL THE WHISTLE BLOWS: A COLLECTION OF GAMES, DANCES, AND ACTIVITIES FOR EIGHT- TO TWELVE-YEAR-OLDS* © 1977 GOODYEAR PUBLISHING COMPANY, INC.

THE MUSCULAR SYSTEM

The human body is composed of some 650 to 700 separate muscles that make up 40 to 60 percent of its total weight. These muscles may be divided into three types:
- **skeletal**—are voluntary and move the body
- **smooth**—are involuntary and form the walls of all internal organs and surround the intestines and blood vessels
- **cardiac**—is involuntary and forms the heart

Muscles cannot push: they can only pull, and in doing so, they shorten or contract. To enable skeletal or voluntary muscles to reverse the moves they make, they are usually arranged in pairs or combinations such as that, for instance, one group pulls the arm forward and up and another group pulls it backward and up. Groups of muscles working together to perform a task are called **synergist**. Those acting in opposition are called **antagonist**.

Within the body, various groups of neighboring muscles work together. Such muscle groups are those of the chest, back, arms, legs, neck, face, foot, and the organs.

Strong muscles are needed to fight off the pull of gravity, to resist fatigue, to look healthy, to move gracefully, to become skilled in sports, and to be a winner in life. Exercise stimulates muscle growth, while the lack of it causes a muscle to diminish in size and strength (**atropy**). Protein is the main cell and muscle builder. It is found in meat, fish, poultry, eggs, milk, cheese, peas, beans, and nuts.

Related Activities:

- Talk about muscles. How can you tell a muscle is growing stronger? Can anyone develop larger muscles? What kinds of exercise promote most muscle growth? How often should you exercise? Does vigorous play stimulate muscle growth?
- What kinds of work can you do around your home to promote muscle growth? Would a hand- or motor-powered lawn mower provide more exercise? When doing errands for your parents, would walking or running provide more exercise?
- What is a muscle cramp? What causes such a cramp? (E.g., chilling, an inadequate supply of blood to the muscle.) What can you do to relieve the pain and stiffness associated with a cramp? (E.g., warm and massage the affected muscle to stimulate the flow of blood to it; stretch it if possible to "loosen" the cramp.)
- What is a "Charley horse"? Did you ever have one?
- Do some of the Stretching and Bending Activities on page 49.

8

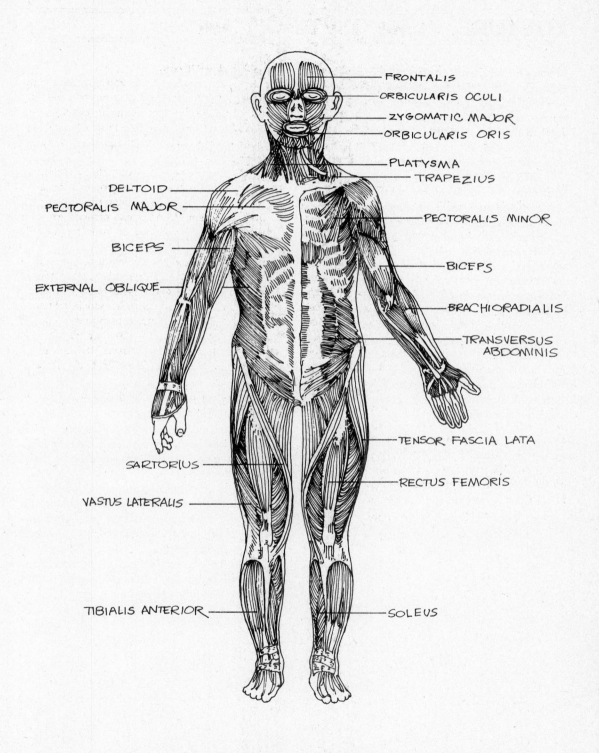

FRONTALIS
ORBICULARIS OCULI
ZYGOMATIC MAJOR
ORBICULARIS ORIS
PLATYSMA
TRAPEZIUS
DELTOID
PECTORALIS MAJOR
PECTORALIS MINOR
BICEPS
BICEPS
EXTERNAL OBLIQUE
BRACHIORADIALIS
TRANSVERSUS ABDOMINIS
TENSOR FASCIA LATA
SARTORIUS
RECTUS FEMORIS
VASTUS LATERALIS
TIBIALIS ANTERIOR
SOLEUS

THE MUSCULAR SYSTEM

POSTURE

Posture is the relative arrangement or position of different parts of the body. **Good posture** keeps all body organs in the position in which they function best and are not crowded by other organs or restricted in their movement. When standing, the head should be held up with the chin slightly tucked. The chest should be raised as if lifted by a string attached to the breastbone (**sternum**), the abdomen should be flat, and the curves of the back should be within normal limits. A straight line drawn vertically should pass through the ear, shoulder, hip, and ankle.

Poor posture is usually caused by muscle weakness or laziness. Among named postural defects are lordosis, kyphosis, and scoliosis. **Lordosis** is abnormal forward curvature of the spine. **Kyphosis**, on the other hand, is abnormal backward curvature of the spine. **Scoliosis**, from the Greek word *skoliosis* meaning crookedness, is lateral curvature of the spine. While these conditions are sometimes congenital, they are often the result of inadequate muscle development or muscle imbalance and may be corrected by carefully prescribed exercises.

Related Activities:

- Talk about the relationship between good posture and good balance.
- Try or review Balance Beam Activities on page 23, Balancing Activities 1 on page 24, Balancing Activities 2 on page 55, the One-Leg Balance on page 118, the Crane Stand on page 156, and the Crane Dive on page 138.
- Use a full-length mirror to enable children to assess their posture while walking, standing, sitting, and lifting.
- If possible, take photographs or motion pictures of children for posture evaluation. This might become a "before" and "after" activity where photographs are taken at the beginning of the year and again after children have been made aware of their posture and have participated in some posture-developing exercises and activities.
- If photographs are out of the question, use a strong light source to cast each child's shadow on white butcher or construction paper and make posture silhouettes.
- Talk about or list occupations in which good posture obviously contributes to success (e.g., being a model, a tightrope walker, a ballet dancer).
- Talk about or list occupations that tend to encourage the development of poor posture by requiring that people stand or sit uncomfortably or bend awkwardly for long periods (e.g., picking cotton).
- Discuss the way furniture that is properly constructed contributes to the development and maintenance of good posture.

8

GOOD   POSTURE

THE CARDIOVASCULAR SYSTEM

The **cardiovascular system** includes the **heart, arteries, veins,** and **blood**. Each person has five to six quarts of blood in his body. The heart, which is about the size of a clinched fist, pumps this blood through the arteries into the capillaries and back through the veins to the heart. During rest, the blood makes one complete journey around the body each minute. During exercise, it may make nine trips in the same amount of time.

The arteries, veins, and capillaries are called **blood vessels**. They are tubes and hoses of varying size through which the body's blood is pumped. If all the blood vessels in one adult human body were hooked end-to-end, they would extend thousands of miles!

The heart is composed of four chambers, the left and right **auricles** and the left and right **ventricles**. **Valves** within the heart control the flow of blood between the chambers.

The blood is made up of red blood cells, white blood cells, platelets, and plasma.

- **Red blood cells**, produced in the bone marrow, carry oxygen and carbon dioxide between the tissues and the lungs.
- **White blood cells**, produced in the bone marrow, the thymus, the spleen, and the lymph nodes, defend the body against infection.
- **Platelets**, disc-shaped blood corpuscles, repair damaged vessels and aid in the blood clotting process.
- **Plasma**, a water-like substance, makes up 50 percent of the blood. It carries nutrients to all cells, removes water products, and acts as a cooling system during exercise.

The development of strong skeletal muscles through exercise usually results in a strong cardiovascular system.

Related Activities:

- Help children feel their pulse in a superficial artery of the wrist or neck. Explain that what they are feeling is the ventricles' strong contraction, what we call the **heartbeat**. Record and compare pulse rates for different children before and after vigorous activity. Normal rates before activity are:

for a baby	130 beats per minute
for a ten-year-old	90 beats per minute
for an adult woman	78 beats per minute
for an adult man	70 beats per minute

- If possible, borrow a stethoscope and help each child listen to his own heartbeat.

- Talk about pumps. What kinds of pumps are there? How do they work? Why are pumps needed? Why can't we rely on water and other liquids to flow down or up, wherever they are needed or wanted? Why does the circulatory system need a pump?

- What happens to the relative distribution of blood throughout the body when you stand on your head, hang by your knees, or otherwise remain for a time with your head below heart level? Why might sitting with his head between his knees help someone who feels dizzy or faint?

- Talk about first aid and the importance of stopping or controlling bleeding. Mention that the flow of blood from minor cuts on the arms and legs can often be slowed to permit natural clotting by elevating the affected part of the body above heart level (i.e., raising your hand over your head or lying down with your leg elevated).

8

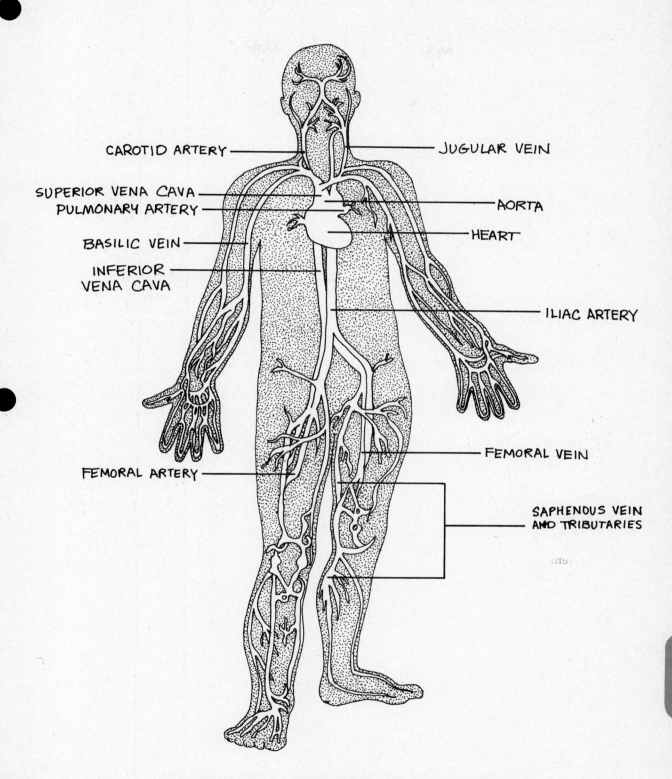

CAROTID ARTERY

JUGULAR VEIN

SUPERIOR VENA CAVA
PULMONARY ARTERY

AORTA

BASILIC VEIN

HEART

INFERIOR
VENA CAVA

ILIAC ARTERY

FEMORAL VEIN

FEMORAL ARTERY

SAPHENOUS VEIN
AND TRIBUTARIES

THE CARDIOVASCULAR SYSTEM

THE LYMPHATIC SYSTEM

The **lymphatic system** is a system of vessels that carry lymph throughout the body. **Lymph** is a watery fluid that drains from the blood vessels and tissues, carrying away waste materials. Little glands called **lymph nodes** serve as filters for this system. As the lymph passes through them, they trap and destroy harmful bacteria. The cleaned lymph is then returned to the bloodstream. The lymphatic system has no pump, but relies instead on body motion to circulate lymph through its vessels.

8

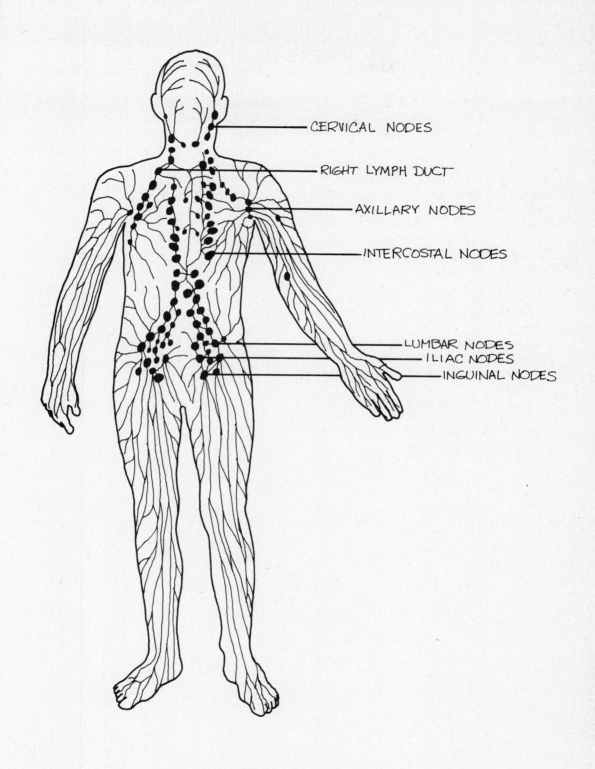

CERVICAL NODES

RIGHT LYMPH DUCT

AXILLARY NODES

INTERCOSTAL NODES

LUMBAR NODES
ILIAC NODES
INGUINAL NODES

THE LYMPHATIC SYSTEM

THE ENDOCRINE SYSTEM

The **endocrine system** consists of ductless glands located in the head, neck, and torso. These glands make and secrete chemical substances called **hormones** that regulate the work of various body organs. Among these glands are:

- the **pituitary**, the master ductless gland, which controls all other glands and regulates body growth.
- the **thyroid**, which regulates body temperature and determines how quickly the body uses up food and oxygen.
- the **parathyroid**, which controls body metabolism.
- the **pancreas**, which produces **insulin**, a substance that helps the muscles convert sugar to energy.
- the **adrenal glands**, which produce **adrenalin**, a substance that speeds up the heartbeat and gives the body added energy in an emergency.
- the **sex glands** or **gonads** (**ovaries** in girls and **testicles** in boys), which stimulate the development of sex specific physical characteristics and are used in reproduction.

Related Activities:
- What is a **duct**?
- If these glands are **ductless**, how do the hormones get out of the glands to do their work in the body?
- What is **osmosis**?

8

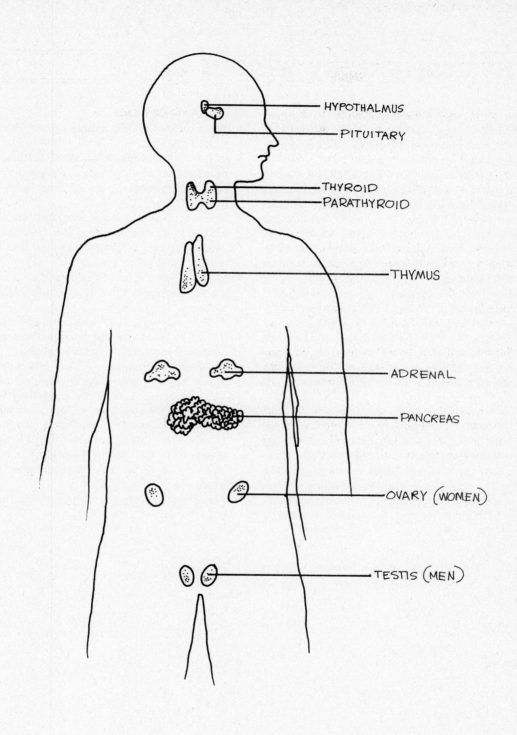

HYPOTHALMUS

PITUITARY

THYROID

PARATHYROID

THYMUS

ADRENAL

PANCREAS

OVARY (WOMEN)

TESTIS (MEN)

THE ENDOCRINE SYSTEM

THE RESPIRATORY SYSTEM

The **respiratory system** includes the **nose, trachea, larynx,** and **lungs**. Its major responsibilities are to bring **oxygen** into the body and to remove **carbon dioxide** from it.

Oxygen is brought into the body in air inhaled through the nose. The hairs and sticky mucous lining of the nose trap dust and other particles that may be in the air so that they do not damage the lungs. The myriad tiny blood vessels in the nose warm the inhaled air as it passes over them so that it is close to body temperature when it enters the lungs.

The exchange of carbon dioxide for oxygen is accomplished in the lungs. The lungs are subdivided into millions of very small, balloon-like air sacs. A network of tiny blood vessels surrounds each air sac. Through these vessels, oxygen passes to the red blood cells, and carbon dioxide is removed from them to be breathed out of the body.

Underneath the lungs is a muscle called the **diaphragm**. When you inhale, it contracts, pulling the ribs up and making room for more air. As you relax to exhale, the rib cage becomes smaller, lung capacity is reduced, and air within the lungs is forced out. When you are sitting still, this process takes place about 18 times each minute. During exercise, it occurs much more frequently.

Related Activities:

- What do **inhale** and **exhale** mean? Demonstrate each one.
- What do the words **expiration, inspiration, perspiration,** and **respiration** have in common? Look them up to see what each one means.
- Talk about how delicate the lungs are, how easily they can be damaged, and how the respiratory system is designed to filter and heat inhaled air to protect them.
- Explain that the body's natural defenses are inadequate against the inhalation of cigarette smoke, polluted air, etc.
- Talk about pollution. How does air become polluted? What are the principal sources of pollutants in the air? What natural objects help clean and purify the air? (Green plants.) What effect does severe air pollution have on them?
- Talk about diseases of the lungs and respiratory system, such as asthma, bronchitis, cancer, emphysema, pneumonia, and tuberculosis. How does each one affect the lungs' ability to do their essential work in the body? How can they be prevented, detected, and treated?
- Talk about posture and its relationship to lung capacity.

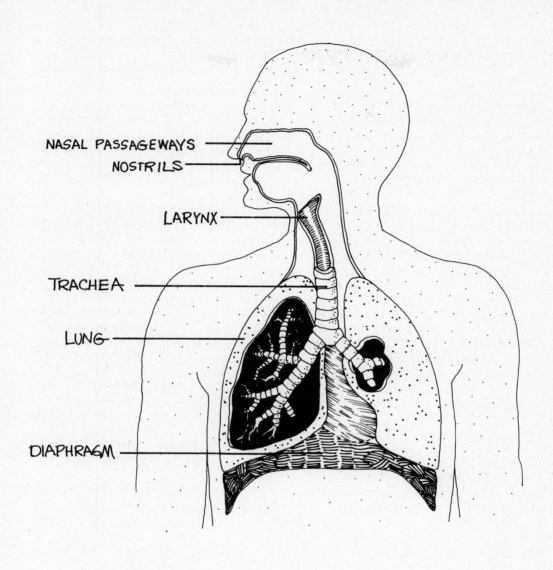

NASAL PASSAGEWAYS

NOSTRILS

LARYNX

TRACHEA

LUNG

DIAPHRAGM

THE RESPIRATORY SYSTEM

THE NERVOUS SYSTEM

The **nervous system** consists of the **brain**, the **spinal cord**, and the **nerves**.

The brain is a complicated communications center. It receives impulses from all parts of the body, deciphers them, and either stores the information they contain or sends a reply to the body to do something. The three main parts of the brain are:

- **cerebrum**—center of thinking and feeling
- **cerebellum**—helps move muscles
- **medulla**—controls automatic body functions, including breathing and heartbeat

The spinal cord, a half-inch-thick cable, runs from the brain all the way down the back through holes in the vertebrae. Two kinds of nerves connect the spinal cord with parts of the body. One kind carries messages from the brain through the spinal cord to the body and the other kind carries messages from the body through the cord to the brain. Some messages do not go all the way to the brain. Instead, they result in a **reflex action** initiated in the spinal cord.

The nervous system may be thought of as two subsystems, the **central nervous system** and the **autonomic nervous system**. The central nervous system controls all voluntary movements, while the autonomic system controls movements you don't have to think about, like the beat of your heart, the breaths that you take, and the reflex actions that quickly move you or parts of your body away from pain or danger.

Related Activities:

- Talk about the brain. How does the skull protect it? Are there joints in the skull? What is a baby's soft spot? Is the human brain relatively large or small compared to the size of the body it directs and controls? What about a dinosaur's brain? Do you think dinosaurs were very smart?

- Talk about nerves. Name several places in the human body that are very sensitive to touch—or are ticklish—because of a heavy concentration of nerve ends (e.g., fingertips, soles of the feet).

- What is **Braille**? How is it used?

- Untwist two paper clips and attach them to a ruler (perhaps with rubber bands) an inch or two apart. Have one child touch some part of another child's body (back, neck, forearm, palm) lightly with this "sensometer." How close together can the paper clips be placed before it is no longer possible to "feel" two distinct points? Does this distance vary from one part of the body to another? From boys to girls? From one person to another? What might this distance indicate about the number of nerve endings in a particular part of the body?

- Conduct some touch tests in which children wear blindfolds and must rely on their sense of touch to identify familiar objects.

8

FROM UNTIL THE WHISTLE BLOWS: A COLLECTION OF GAMES, DANCES, AND ACTIVITIES FOR EIGHT- TO TWELVE-YEAR-OLDS ©1977 GOODYEAR PUBLISHING COMPANY, INC.

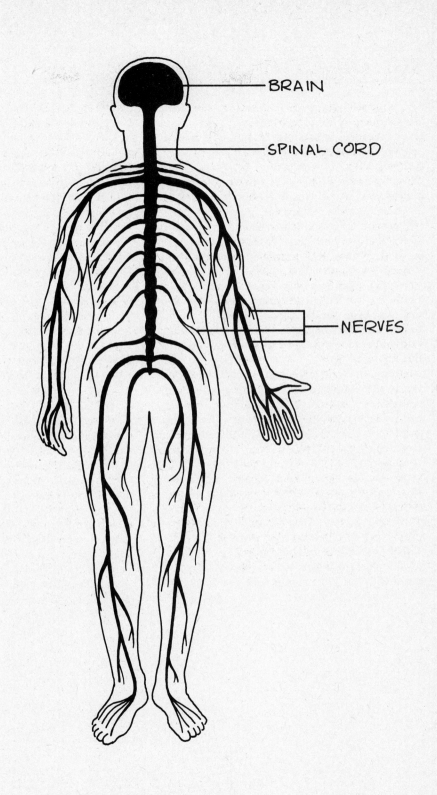

BRAIN

SPINAL CORD

NERVES

THE NERVOUS SYSTEM

THE DIGESTIVE SYSTEM

The **digestive system** includes the **mouth, esophagus, stomach, small intestine**, and **large intestine**, which form a long tube extending from the mouth to the **anus** or **rectum**. The system's function is to take in food and water, make them usable for body growth and repair, and eliminate the waste products. This food processing is called **digestion**.

Digestion begins in the mouth. Your sharp **teeth** (incisors and cuspids) bite off pieces of food. Your broader, flatter teeth (bicuspids and molars) chew and grind it. As your teeth chew your food, three sets of **salivary glands** in your mouth secrete **saliva** to moisten the food and help you taste it. **Taste buds** located on your tongue tell you whether the food is sweet, sour, bitter, or salty. Your sense of smell tells you it's fried chicken!

During the chewing process, your **tongue** moves the food around in your mouth, then pushes it to the back of your mouth to be swallowed. Swallowed food goes down the esophagus into the stomach. Located under your ribs on the left side of your abdomen, the stomach is like a J-shaped balloon made of tough muscle rather than rubber. **Sphincter muscles** close both stomach openings so that food will not be squeezed back up into the esophagus or down into the small intestine before it is ready. Glands in the stomach walls secrete digestive juices. These juices contain special chemical substances called **enzymes** that are mixed with the food by the squeezing action of the stomach-wall muscles and aid in breaking it down.

After about three hours, the sphincter leading to the small intestine opens, and contracting stomach muscles push the food into the intestinal tract. Together, the small and large intestines are about 30 feet long. They have to be coiled up like a garden hose to fit within your body. Strong muscles developed through daily exercise aid in pushing food along in the intestines.

In the small intestine, additional digestive juices from the **liver, gall bladder**, and **pancreas** are added, muscles continue mixing and pushing the food, and tiny blood vessels absorb useful food particles into the bloodstream. The large intestine absorbs any useful liquid remaining in the food mixture and eliminates what is left through the rectum as semisolid waste.

Related Activities:

- Why does food lose its "taste" when your nose is "stopped up" as the result of a cold or allergies?
- Conduct some taste tests in which children wear blindfolds and hold their noses (briefly) so that they are forced to rely on their taste buds alone. (*Note:* A bite of bland cracker or a swish of water will help eliminate residual effects from an old taste so that a new one can be appreciated.)
- Using simple substances (e.g., table sugar and salt, a lemon slice, and an orange peel), help children identify sweet, salty, sour, and bitter tastes. Can they distinguish between salt and sugar using taste alone?
- Why is it unwise to exercise vigorously or swim shortly after eating a large meal?

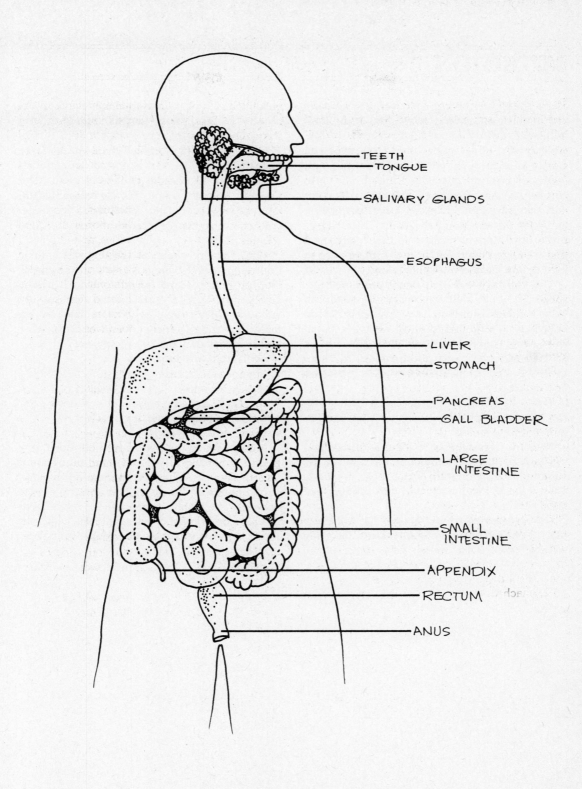

TEETH
TONGUE
SALIVARY GLANDS
ESOPHAGUS
LIVER
STOMACH
PANCREAS
GALL BLADDER
LARGE INTESTINE
SMALL INTESTINE
APPENDIX
RECTUM
ANUS

THE DIGESTIVE SYSTEM

NUTRITION

Many American children are overweight, many are malnourished, and some are both! Malnourished children may have pale skin, dull-looking hair, circles under their eyes, flabby or stringy muscles, a flat chest, thin arms and legs, and poor posture. They often find it difficult to concentrate and frequently fall victim to colds and skin infections. In many instances, obesity and malnutrition share the same cause: ignorance or a nutrient negligence that maintains it doesn't matter what you fill the stomach with so long as you do fill it at regular intervals.

The truth is, the body's needs are simple but specific: if bones are being built or repaired, calcium is needed, and carbohydrates will *not* do equally well—will not do at all! Children should learn early what the body's nutritional needs are so they can make wise food choices to better meet the needs of their own bodies as they grow and develop.

The body's basic nutrients may be divided into five categories: proteins, carbohydrates, fats, vitamins, and minerals.

Protein is essential to building and maintaining each body cell. In addition, it aids in the development of antibodies which help the body resist disease. Meat, eggs, and milk products are good sources of protein.

Carbohydrates supply energy for work and play. If one's diet lacks carbohydrates, the body will use proteins for energy rather than for cell building and repair. Carbohydrates are found in breads, cereals, fruits, sweets, potatoes, and some other vegetables.

Fats are used both as fuel and as insulation to help the body maintain a normal temperature (98.6°). The fat content of food is often measured in calories, a unit that expresses the energy- or heat-producing value of the food. Bacon, cream, butter, and some meats are good sources of fat.

Vitamins are chemical substances found in both animal and vegetable matter. In general, they promote normal growth, maintain health, and prevent and/or cure certain diseases. An adequate daily supply of vitamins may be obtained by eating a variety of basic foods, such as:

- leafy green and yellow vegetables
- citrus fruits and tomatoes
- potatoes and fruits
- cheese and milk
- meat, fish, poultry, eggs, and legumes
- butter and margarine
- breads and cereals

Minerals help the body resist infections, promote the healing of wounds, and aid in curing various illnesses. They are essential for building strong bones and teeth, and for having a good appetite. The main minerals needed by the body are calcium, phosphorous, and iron, which are found in most leafy green vegetables, fruits, liver, and kidneys.

THE BODY'S VITAMIN AND MINERAL NEEDS

Name	Source	Function in the Body	Servings Daily
Vitamin A	Butter, cheese, cod liver oil, egg yolk, leafy green vegetables, liver, yellow vegetables, and tomatoes	Promotes normal vision and growth; maintains general health	One
Vitamin B Complex	Lean pork, liver, egg yolk, whole grains, beans, peas, nuts, fruits, vegetables	Stimulates appetite; aids digestion; promotes growth; regulates nervous system	Two
Vitamin C	Citrus fruits, other fresh fruits, berries, cabbage, greens, fresh vegetables, sprouted legumes	Maintains connective tissue; assists in the development of bones and teeth; aids cell activity; strengthens blood vessels and body tissues	Two (cannot be stored)
Vitamin D	Eggs, liver, fish, sunshine	Essential for bone and teeth development; promotes growth	One
Vitamin E	Egg yolk, cereals, lettuce, spinach, corn oil	Promotes general well-being, mental and physical vigor, good muscle tone	One
Calcium	Almonds, cheese, dry beans, egg yolk, milk, leafy vegetables, molasses	Assists in the development of bones and teeth; aids blood clotting; essential for healthy muscles and nerves	Two
Copper	Avocadoes, dry beans, peas, liver, oats, corn, whole wheat	Aids cell activity; prevents certain anemias	One
Iodine	Seafoods, fish, foods grown near the ocean, iodized salt	Encourages normal growth; prevents goiter	One
Iron	Berries, fruits, dried fruits, dried beans, peas, eggs, lean meats, bread, green vegetables, molasses, rye flour, whole wheat, oatmeal	Builds hemoglobin and other carriers of oxygen; prevents some anemias	One
Phosphorus	Cheese, dried beans, liver, nuts, flour	Stimulates and aids cell activity; assists in the development of bones and teeth	One
Potassium	Dried apricots, dates, figs, dried beans, molasses, nuts, soy flour	Promotes growth; stimulates and aids cell activity; essential for healthy heart, nerves, and muscles	One
Sodium	Bread, butter, cheese, salmon, table salt	Helps maintain water balance; prevents fatigue	One

8

DISEASES

A **disease** is an abnormal condition of an organism as a consequence of infection, inherent weakness, or environmental factors which impairs normal functioning. Some diseases, such as pellagra, rickets,and scurvy, are caused by deficiencies of certain vitamins and minerals. Other diseases, such as colds, measles, mumps, and chicken pox, are caused by germs.

Germs or **microbes** destroy body cells and produce poisons that can make the body very sick. They are especially dangerous because, once inside the body, they grow and reproduce rapidly. Some become fully grown within a few minutes. Among these disease-causing organisms are bacteria, protozoa, and viruses.

Bacteria are one-celled microorganisms found everywhere. Most of them are harmless and are essential for plant growth; however,a few of them cause infections, blood poisoning, food spoilage, pneumonia, whooping cough, typhoid, and scarlet fever.

Protozoa are tiny animals that live in the water. Most of them are helpful, but a few cause diseases such as malaria and sleeping sickness.

Viruses are submicroscopic bacteria or fungi that cause colds, influenza, measles, mumps, chicken pox, and polio. Diseases caused by viruses do not respond well to medication and are, for the most part, easier to prevent than to cure.

Resistance to germs may be developed by
- getting plenty of rest, exercising, and eating the correct foods;
- keeping clean and treating all wounds;
- washing your hands before eating;
- keeping warm and dry, avoiding becoming chilled;
- staying away from people who are sick;
- drinking only purified liquids and eating only unspoiled foods;

- visiting your doctor and dentist regularly for checkups and following their advice.

Disease is spread most often
- person to person by coughs or sneezes;
- by insects, such as flies, cockroaches, and mosquitos, or by fungi;
- by the bite of an infected animal (dog, cat, or parasite);
- by drinking unpastuerized milk or polluted water, or by eating meat from an infected animal;
- by human carriers who are immune to the disease's effects and so may not know they are carrying it.

THE BODY'S DEFENSES

The body's defenses include its covering, its white blood cells, and its temperature. The **skin** is the body's first line of defense. It should be kept clean; breaks in it, such as scratches and cuts, should be cleansed and treated with an antiseptic solution. If deep or extensive, they should also be covered. The **white blood cells** form a second line of defense: they surround and destroy germs. Another of the body's defenses is **temperature elevation**: some bacteria cannot live at the high temperatures we call a fever and thus are destroyed.

In response to infection or exposure to disease, the body may develop **antibodies**, chemical substances within the bloodstream that kill invading germs. The production of antibodies within the body can be stimulated by the injection of **antigens** or **haptens**, that is, by "shots" or vaccination.

If the disease is prolonged or severe, or the body's defenses prove inadequate, the doctor may need to give medicine to help the body fight off the germs' effects.

SAFETY AND ACCIDENT PREVENTION

Every year thousands of children lose their lives, are permanently injured, or miss time from school because of accidents. To prevent accidents, anticipate them and take corrective action before they happen.

1. Develop safety patrols to prevent jaywalking, dashing into the street, crossing the streets outside crosswalks, and playing in unsafe areas. See that traffic in corridors or on stairways moves in an orderly fashion.

2. Provide instruction on where and how to use roller skates, skate boards, scooters, and bicycles, and where to store them.

3. Inspect daily for maintenance defects and housekeeping carelessness in buildings and play areas. Among other things, check
   - exit lights
   - exit door locks
   - electrical connections
   - fire extinguishers
   - stair treads and handrails (Are there splinters or exposed nails?)
   - floors (Are they slippery?)
   - playground equipment

4. Encourage everyone to report all accidents on an accident report form and to list the probable cause. Follow up on all probable causes to assure that remedial action is taken so that the same accident will not recur.

5. Have readily available *all* telephone numbers that might be needed in an emergency, such as those of the
   - fire department
   - physician
   - nurse
   - emergency hospital
   - parents or guardians at home and at work

6. Conduct regular fire, safety, and disaster drills. Discuss with children *exactly* what they should do in such emergencies, and in what order.

7. All games have dangerous elements. Teach children how to avoid being hit, being run into, or running into someone; how to fall; and how to protect themselves by being alert to dangers and by raising their hands, tucking, ducking, or taking other evasive action. Teach them not to throw bats, masks, or other equipment, or rocks, bottles, sticks, and other objects.

8. Encourage children to be safety conscious and to correct or report dangerous situations they observe (e.g., a busy intersection where a traffic light or crossing guard is needed, a loose rung or bar on playground equipment, broken glass or other sharp objects scattered about a play area).

CONCLUSION

The human body is a miraculous structure in which many diverse building blocks are combined to make possible work and play. The simplest of these blocks is the **cell**. Within the body, cells are combined to make **tissues**, tissues to make **organs**, and organs to make **systems**. All nine of the body's major systems work together to keep it alive and functioning properly. Children need to learn early how to nourish, exercise, and relax their bodies and how to protect them from accidents and disease. Adults who work with children have an inescapable responsibility to teach these lessons through study and activity and by example.

8

BIBLIOGRAPHY

Anderson, M. H., et al., *Play with a Purpose* (New York: Harper and Row, 1966).

Braga, Laurie, and Joseph Braga, *Learning and Growing: A Guide to Child Development* (Englewood Cliffs, N.J.: Prentice-Hall, 1975).

Byrd, O. E., et al., *Health-6: Health, Safety, Fitness* (Sacramento: California State Department of Education, 1967).

_____ et al., *Health-7: Health, Safety, Fitness* (River Forest, Ill.: Laidlaw, 1966).

Callaghan, J., *Soccer* (Pacific Palisades, Calif.: Goodyear, 1969).

Corbin, C. B., *Becoming Physically Educated in the Elementary School* (Philadelphia, Pa.: Lea and Febiger, 1969).

Dauer, V. P., *Essential Movement Experiences for Preschool and Primary Children* (Minneapolis, Minn.: Burgess, 1972).

_____ and R. P. Pangrazi, *Dynamic Physical Education for Elementary School Children* (5th ed.; Minneapolis, Minn.: Burgess, 1975).

Dawson, H. L., *Basic Human Anatomy* (New York: Appleton-Century-Crofts, 1966).

Dexter, G., *The Physical Performance Test for California* (rev.; Sacramento: California State Department of Education, 1971).

Fait, Gregory, and Gerry Fait, *Physical Education for the Elementary School Child* (3rd ed.; Philadelphia, Pa.: W. B. Saunders, 1976).

Fraser, E. D., et al., *The Child and Physical Education* (Englewood Cliffs, N.J.: Prentice-Hall, 1956).

Hall, J. T. *Folk Dance* (Pacific Palisades, Calif.: Goodyear, 1969).

_____, *Dance: A Complete Guide to Social, Folk and Square Dancing* (Belmont, Calif.: Wadsworth, 1963).

_____, *School Recreation: Its Organization, Supervision and Administration* (Dubuque, Iowa: Wm. C. Brown, 1966).

_____, et al., *Fundamentals of Physical Education* (Pacific Palisades, Calif.: Goodyear, 1969).

Holt, J., *How Children Learn* (New York: Pitman, 1967).

Kimber, D. C., et al., *Textbook of Anatomy and Physiology* (New York: Macmillan, 1942).

Latchaw, M., and G. Egstrom, *Human Movement* (Englewood Cliffs, N.J.: Prentice-Hall, 1969).

Lauber, P., *Your Body and How It Works* (New York: Random House, 1962).

Miller, A. G., and V. Whitcomb, *Physical Education in the Elementary School Curriculum* (3rd ed.; Englewood Cliffs, N.J.: Prentice-Hall, 1969).

Neilson, N. P., and W. Van Hagen, *Physical Education for Elementary Schools* (New York: A. S. Barnes, 1954).

Perry, R. H., *Men's Basketball* (Pacific Palisades, Calif.: Goodyear, 1969).

Physical Education Teaching Guide, Grades Three, Four, Five, Six, Division of Instructional Services, Publication No. 537 (Los Angeles: Los Angeles City Schools, 1961).

Richardson, H. A., *Games for the Elementary School Grades* (Minneapolis, Minn.: Burgess, 1951).

Safrit, M., *Evaluation in Physical Education: Assessing Motor Behavior* (Englewood Cliffs, N.J.: Prentice-Hall, 1973).

Sandefur, R., *Volleyball* (Pacific Palisades, Calif.: Goodyear, 1970).

Schurr, E. L., *Movement Experiences for Children: Curriculum and Methods for Elementary School Physical Education* (New York: Appleton-Century-Crofts, 1967).

Smith, J. W., et al., *Outdoor Education* (2nd ed.; Englewood Cliffs, N.J.: Prentice-Hall, n.d.).

Stallings, L. M., *Motor Skills, Development and Learning* (Dubuque, Iowa: Wm. C. Brown, 1973).

Stutts, A., *Women's Basketball* (Pacific Palisades, Calif.: Goodyear, 1969).

Vannier, M., and M. Foster, *Teaching Physical Education in Elementary Schools* (Philadelphia, Pa.: W. B. Saunders, 1968).

Wallis, E. L., and G. A. Logan, *Exercise for Children* (Englewood Cliffs, N.J.: Prentice-Hall, 1966).

Wilson, C. C., and E. A. Wilson, *Health and Living, Teachers' Guide* (New York: Bobbs-Merrill, 1965).

INDEX OF ACTIVITIES AND TERMS

INDEX OF SKILLS